IMAGES
*of Scotland*

# AROUND
# DOUNE AND
# DEANSTON

John e Angela

Good Luck.

*Karen*

Stobie's map of Kilmadock Parish as it was in 1783. It shows a great number of old spellings and identifies places that do not exist today as well as places that have moved to a different location. Sight of the full copy is a must for the enthusiast. Kilmadock is the name of the ancient monastery, which was established on the banks of the Teith at Old Kilmadock where the Annat meets the Teith. The name is taken from the saint Docus who died in the sixth century AD, hence the link, but there is still much to be learned about the origins of that ancient site.

IMAGES
*of Scotland*

# AROUND
# DOUNE AND
# DEANSTON

*Karen Ross*

TEMPUS

*This book is dedicated to my mother,*
*Anna Gillies MacEwan,*
*who loved nothing better*
*than to romance with the past,*
*something I have only learned to do,*
*regrettably, with her passing.*

First published 2002
Copyright © Karen Ross, 2002

Tempus Publishing Limited
The Mill, Brimscombe Port,
Stroud, Gloucestershire, GL5 2QG
www.tempus-publishing.com

ISBN 0 7524 2768 7

TYPESETTING AND ORIGINATION BY
Tempus Publishing Limited
PRINTED IN GREAT BRITAIN BY
Midway Colour Print, Wiltshire

# Contents

# Foreword

It is with great pleasure that I write the foreword to Karen Ross's book on Doune and Deanston. Karen kept me informed of the book's progress over many months and it was soon evident that her hard work, imagination and enthusiasm has produced a fascinating and evocative image of Kilmadock parish over the ages.

Within these pages the past is reawakened and memories of Sweetie Sandy, the Grosset Fair and the Gala Queen live on. The parish has a timeless enduring quality that contrasts with the energy and bustle that has flowed through it between Highlands and Lowlands over the centuries – a rock on the shore over which the ebb and flow of time and history have passed.

I am full of admiration for the hours of research and hard work put into the preparation of this book, with its wonderful collection of old photographs, which I feel sure will give much enjoyment not only to local people but to a wider public as well.

Lord Doune
18 June 2002

The celebrations for Lord Doune's coming of age in 1913; the children's parade from Main Street to the castle.

# Introduction

This little book is a light pictorial account of these villages over the last 150 years or so with a reminder that, in fact, some of the area's oldest known history has only recently been discovered. I hope the book is easily digestible and enjoyable, and that it gives the reader a sense of the history and importance of these communities in central Scotland. It depicts a slower pace of life when maybe people were more in tune with their environments in the ways in which they worked and socialised, and how they interacted more in the community. One great bonus for me in putting this book together has been the new friends I have made, who form part of the communities and who, in the normal course of events, I would probably never know. This has brought home to me how our lifestyle today inhibits the interaction that is necessary to keep a real sense of community alive and how hard it can be to overcome the restraints of modern life and get out and about!

Doune, with its fort and castle, and Deanston, with the mill which once employed over 1,000 people, illustrate the importance of this area on the Highland fringe. A unique culture evolved with this strategic importance.

Gateway to the Central Highlands from the Forth and Teith crossings, it may have been a more prosperous community than some, but it was still a fragile community evolving through these trade links. Luxuries would be few; death in childbirth and infant mortality were commonplace. For many, a hand-to-mouth existence was gained mainly from the land and occasional bartering. The area had a few rambling mansions for the gentry but more 'but and bens' for the majority. Doune, in particular, was a scattered community of unrelated dwellings and not the ordered route we see today.

Deanston, a hidden community evolving with many claims to fame through the Mill, became, in a short time, a fine example of order and mechanical advancement. It had a cared for workforce, enjoying the best of its day, and claiming to be the first village in Britain to have gas.

I (like the reader I suspect) have fallen in love with the Braes of Doune and the Vale of the Teith. I am enchanted by its history and its beauty, still in unspoiled relief, which allows the mind to imagine easily the life of the souls that lived here. I have lived all over the place but my associations with this area are inbred from childhood. One of my grandmothers came from Cambuskenneth, and my great-grandfather, William Aitken, sailed for Australia in the gold rush never to be heard from again. So many people who now live across the seven seas have links with this area, which go back generations, but they still return either in thought or body to a land they love. Those of us who do live here are really lucky to live daily with the magic and the beauty of the environs of Kilmadock.

If you would like to contribute to recording the area's local history, the Kilmadock Historical Society would be happy to receive or copy any photographs or memorabilia to preserve for future generations. They can be contacted c/o Kilmadock Development Trust at 52 Main Street, Doune, FK16 6BW.

# Acknowledgements

If you are reading this and you helped me in some way, however small, I thank you sincerely. This book belongs to you and the people of the communities. It has, I know, taken a while to produce, but with my family and work commitments it has been hard at times to keep going but so much goodwill and encouragement has spurred me on to the finishing line.

I came to producing this book by accident and it was only while trying to persuade my sister, Morag Lloyds, to produce a book on this area similar to her *Trossachs* book that things backfired. I was trying to say that Doune and Deanston always miss out in the attention stakes, and that with such a historic and significantly beautiful area it was not fair! That is what happens when you complain! I have to say that the biggest acknowledgement has to go to Morag who pointed the publishers in my direction, and for her encouragement and support in all sorts of ways in keeping me going.

Others have been very supportive and generous in sharing their memorabilia. I hope I have remembered all of you; please forgive me if I haven't as you can see that this is quite a list! In no particular order:

Dr N. Reid; University of Saint Andrews Library for permission to reproduce Valentine postcards; Alister and Penny Dickson; John and Isa Calder, who gave so much background information with humour and the most amazing memories. Sadly Isa died while I was compiling this book. Lynn and Niall Bowser; Sandy Rae; Ruth Diffin; John McLaren; Jimuck, who was always helpful (and who passed away just as the book went to press); Nancy Fox; Alison McAlpine; Maidie Finlayson; Harry Doy; David Cameron; Thea Milne; Margaret Ann Dow; Mrs Taylor (who sadly died while I was compiling this book); Jimmy Innes; Gavin Miller; James Kirk; Peter Wordie; Jim 'Tiger' Shaw; Carl Hunter; Daisy Clarke; Barbara Ross (my lovely mother-in-law, who passed away in July 2002); Jimmy McIntosh, who gave me the first wonderful photograph of the Horses at the Bridge of Balkerach; Harvey MacNaughton; Kenny Lauder; John and Cathy Meek; Joyce and Tom Johnston; Bill Inglis; Bob McCutcheon (a well-known local historian, he passed away in August 2002); Treesa Lie; Moira Lawson for keeping me going; Elma Lindsay, Local History Officer at The Smith Art Gallery and Museum, Stirling; Linda Fox; Angus Stroyan; Don Watson; Harvey Murdoch; Henry MacKenzie; Ken Russell; Clark McIntosh; Sue Harvey; George Ince; William and David Forbes; Chrissie Ziolkowski; Iain Morrison; Iain Mathieson; Nigel Bishop, who helped with research and corrections; Diana Bishop; Willie Docherty; Min Croy; Bill Swaine; John Blackwood; Captain D. Bowser; Marian White; Moira Robertson; Mrs Marshall Deanston, Primary Headteacher; Charlie Lockhart and Margaret Lockhart; Margo Bain; Willie Jenkins; Caroline and Colin Stroyan; Alister Buchannan; Lord and Lady Doune; The Earl and Countess of Moray; Di Campbell; Skyview aerial photography; H. Mailer (Whyler Photographers); Royal Commission on the Ancient and Historic Monuments of Scotland; Professor Gordon Maxwell; the publishers, Tempus, in particular Campbell McCutcheon for his patience, support and encouragement. Last but not least my family, Eddie my husband and to my daughter Laura, who was my 'assistant', and a special thanks to my son Stuart who tolerated the inconveniences that putting this book together brought to the Ross household on the Braes of Doune.

# One
# Doune & the Roman Fort

The Romans of Doune were probably not as distinctive as this, having longer 'skirts' and leggings to protect them from the Scottish weather and the midge. Maybe it was the midges that sent them back to Rome!

The copyright of illustrations of the Romans in Doune and the Doune Fairs is owned by Don Watson, who gave so generously of his time and skill to reproduce some of the life of the parish that has disappeared with time.

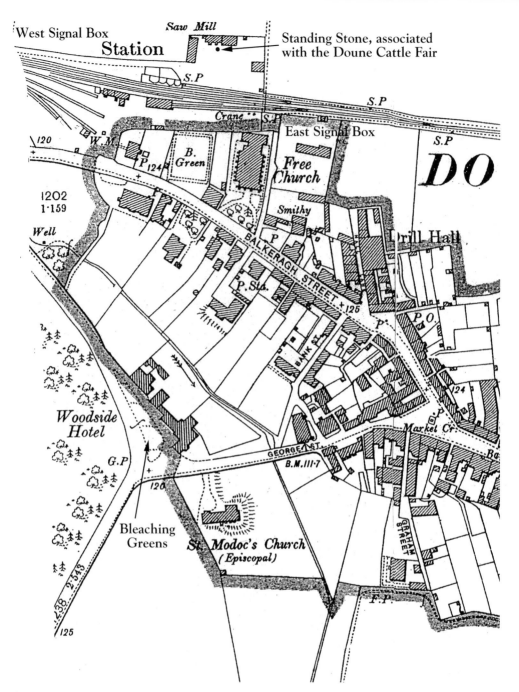

This section of a 1900 map, which is still in print, is worth studying in detail. It shows so many changes it is difficult to itemise them all. Some points of interest are: the old bowling green at Potters field, the old saw mill at the entrance to what is now the Ponds, the railway station and the sidings, and the track, or right of way, which went across the railway line on to the grazing and to the round 'Bluebell Wood', from beside the well on Balkerach Street. You can see the garden of Mile End, which was the first formal bowling green in Doune.

The full-size map shows the old curling pond on the Lundie Burn behind the Black Park and the Sandpit Wood. It is also interesting to note that it shows a significant island in the Teith,

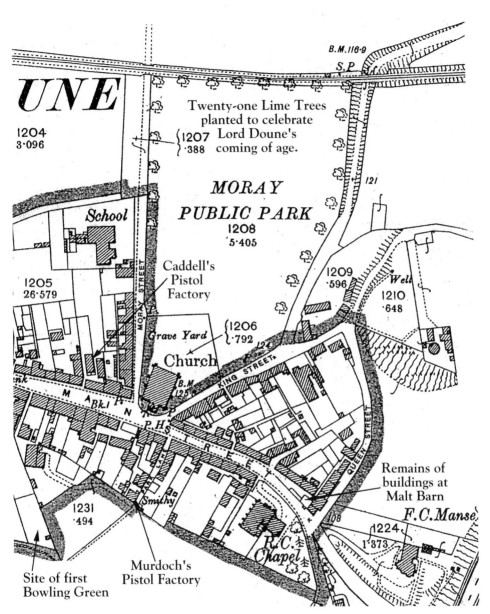

UNE

1204
3·096

Twenty-one Lime Trees
planted to celebrate
{1207 Lord Doune's
·388 coming of age.

121

*School*

MORAY
PUBLIC PARK
1208
·5·405

1205
26·579

Caddell's
Pistol
Factory

MORAY STREET

1209
·596

Well

1210
·648

{1206
·792

*Grave Yard*

Church

B.M.

MARKET STREET

KING STREET

M   A
Bk.I
N

P.H.S

QUEEN STREET

Remains of
buildings at
Malt Barn

*Smithy*

F.C.Manse

1231
·494

1224
1·373

R.C.
Chapel

Site of first
Bowling Green

Murdoch's
Pistol Factory

B.M.116·9
S.P.

starting below the Bridge of Teith Cottage and extending 150 yards or so downstream, the area of one of the fords. There is no Muir Crescent, Muir Hall or War Memorial, no Rural Hall, no Moray flats, nor council houses at Queen Street, Northlea or Castlehill, no school at Castlehill, and the only access to that area of grazing being via Park Lane. Amazingly, no one knew then about the Roman Fort, and the car was a new, rare and noisy thing that travelled too fast at 20mph! A recently opened water supply from the Annat Burn had improved life considerably. Life was horse and cart orientated and no tarmac graced the local roads, only dust and road scrapers – and water sprayers to dampen the dust!

This is what Doune would have looked like from the castle about 1900, with Umvar in the background and the gentle sloping Braes of Doune, foothills of the Grampians, which would have been thickly forested in the days of the Roman occupation. The 'Roman Fort' is hidden under the grass in the centre of the scene, no-one in the days that this photograph was taken was aware of its existence as it was not re-discovered until 1983. The 'castlekeepers' cottage is in the foreground and was once one of many dwellings outwith the castle. The tower of the East Church and the spire of the Free Church can be seen clearly, and under a magnifying glass a lot of the detail contained in the previous map can be made out.

# Doune

Nestling at the foot of the southern most slopes of the Grampians, Doune and its Braes sits to the northeasterly side of the River Teith. Often overlooked for its historical importance because of its unpretentious appearance, it is dominated by a magnificent castle, which while it entices the visitor on the east and west approaches, seems to disappear once in the village. The origins of the name Doune – a hill, mound·or dun – have been much debated. It was always considered slightly inappropriate because of the location of the castle and the original settlements in that area. However, with the discovery of the Roman fort on the hill overlooking the Teith in 1983, the name may now seem more fitting. It may well be that in years to come excavations show other earlier settlements in this area.

This interesting photograph taken in the early days of the twentieth century will be unrecognisable to most. It is Doune taken from the old golf course near the Black Park and Currachmore woods at the foot of the Braes. Taken before the gravel pit was dug and evolved into the ponds we know today, it shows clearly the area used for the Doune Fairs, and makes the appreciation of its suitability easily understood. The old railway station buildings can be seen, the West Church spire and the Kilmadock church tower and four spires, and there in the background the castle casts its protective shadow – a scene from the past as now there is no West Church spire and no spires on the Kilmadock church.

*Opposite:* The view is taken from the western edge of the Black Park wood, known locally as Morrisons Hill. The Merrie walk, which P.C. Merrie did much to establish, is now known as the 'commonty'. This scene shows the road up to Mansfield and West Lundie, before the pilings were established in the days of sheaves and stooks when the original small sandpit was at the edge of the wood. The major sandpit, which was to result in the formation of Doune Ponds, was not yet planned. The Rural Hall can be easily seen in Northlea, with the station buildings behind the haystacks and the old school at the top of Moray Street. In the distance are the Campsie Fells, the Gargunnock and Fintry Hills.

A roman scene at Doune 'Flavian' Fort.

# The Romans in Doune

It is strange that some of the oldest known historical facts about Doune have only been discovered recently. In fact, if it were not for the trained and expert eyes of one Gordon Maxwell we may well still not be aware that the Romans indeed built a fort in Doune. We must not forget that the remains of a child found in a stone cist in the Round Wood were dated to the early Bronze Age *c.*1800 BC. This wood was lost when the sand and gravel quarry carved out what now remains as the Ponds. Local people fondly remember a beauty spot renowned for its bluebells in spring. There are a number of brochs in the area dating from [the first century AD, the most notable of which is Coldoch. During the early 1990s an archaeological study of part of the 'high' Doune Braes revealed evidence of a great deal of early human habitation including hut circles, cairns and farmsteads. Glenhead, Severie and Uamh Bheag are just a few of the local areas revealing Neolithic associations.

To return to the Romans: on 16 August 1983 Gordon Maxwell was undertaking an aerial survey programme for the Royal Commission on the Ancient Monuments of Scotland, one of the objectives of which was to try and establish where the Roman roads crossed the Forth. Inevitably this brought the aircraft above Doune Castle and the old Teith crossing while surveying the Ochtertyre, Blairdrummond and Keir roads. It was a matter of chance that, at about midday, he just happened to look at the ground around the primary school. It was some minutes before he registered what he had just seen. During this exceptionally dry summer spell there was the outline of the distinctive parrot beak entrance and ditches that protected the fort.

The photograph on the next page shows the area of the fort from the air and the superimposed lines show its probable location. The buildings were constructed mainly from timber and earth. All of the school and much of Castlehill may lie within this area and it seems amazing that such development did not invite past builders to ask questions about what they were disturbing. No doubt finance and red tape were responsible. It is a Flavian fort, dating to around AD 80, and was probably occupied by up to 500 Roman soldiers spanning a relatively short twenty years. It is estimated that it covered an area of about 2.8 hectares. The Headland Trust excavated part of the site in September 1999. They established an area that may well be interpreted as a 'hospital'. Six bread ovens were also discovered, which could well have supported 500 men. Also found were rubbish tips and part of a 6m-wide internal service road; more detailed evaluation is awaited. The excavation covered only a very small area of the fort; the footprint of the proposed new nursery school building that required an archaeological evaluation before developers began work.

In time, more about the fort will be discovered and it is not impossible that a watchtower or fortlet also exists in this area, which would link in with the Glenbank to Bertha 'line'. What is now established is that Doune was an important part of the Roman Empire, and the fort, situated on a plateau on the banks of the Teith, would have controlled the crossing and was of significant strategic importance.

The area of the fort as taken in the first aerial shot of the site. The Doune fort is described as a 'route-blocker'. The finding of this fort has resulted in the need for some re-evaluation of the Flavians' strategic plan and the latest analysis is not yet completed. (Photograph reproduced by kind permission of RCAHMS, who retain copyright.)

Aerial view of Doune, showing the fort area in the centre. This picture gives a clear understanding of the strategic importance of the site from every perspective. The top of the picture shows the Doune Ponds on the left, which was the area of the Doune Fairs and, later, the golf course. The lime trees around the Moray Park are distinctive at the top right. (Skyviews 1995. Copies can be obtained from jennie@skyviewsarchives.com)

# Two

# Doune Castle
# & Doune Pistols

## The Castle

Doune is probably best known for its superb medieval castle built around 1419. Some say it was begun around the 1390s. Either way it is one of the best examples of the Scottish Baronial style still standing. Built by Robert, Duke of Albany, Earl of Menteith, and his son, it is unique in that not only is most of the stonework original, but it was built in a single generation. It is also widely acknowledged that the castle was never fully completed and that the west range and the south range were intended to house apartments, as is evident by the rows of fine windows. It is very likely that some form of habitation has been on this site since the earliest settlements in Scotland. Some of the earliest settlements in Doune are thought to have been in the area near the castle on the banks of the Ardoch Burn.

The castle became a royal household in 1425 when James I used it as a hunting lodge. It was in 1503 when Margaret, daughter of Henry VII of England, was gifted the castle that the association with the Earls of Moray was born and which continues to this day. The castle was used for a short period when Queen Mary was in exile. Sir James Stewart became Lord Doune in 1570 and his son married Lady Elizabeth Stewart, elder daughter of the regent Moray, in 1580. In 1592 he was created Earl of Moray by James VI and the castle was frequently used as a hunting lodge. Montrose occupied it in 1645, and in 1654 it was the scene of a skirmish between Mungo Murray and the Cromwellian cavalry. It was seized in 1745 during the Jacobite rebellion and used as a prison to incarcerate government troops, some of whom escaped from Queen Mary's room.

*Opposite:* The castle lies just south-south-west of the Roman Fort and it occupies a similar strategic site on a narrow peninsula between the River Teith and its tributary, the Ardoch Burn. Here you see the Teith on one of its quieter days, just south of the crossing. On the extreme left of the picture you see the top of the embankment on which stood the Roman Fort. It may well be that this site was used for earlier strongholds and it is likely that the origins of Doune village would have been centered on this location close to the favoured Teith crossing where the Highlands meet the Lowlands.

Doune Castle – A castle of which to be proud. It has been described sometimes as 'a real castle, not a group of houses surrounded by a high wall.'

This unusual view from the battlements illustrates the proximity of the Highland line with Ben Ledi in the background. The Teith Bridge can just be seen spanning the river below Deanston House. Deanston village is hidden in the trees.

Doune Castle from Bridge of Teith.

This scene illustrates a time when the castle was used briefly in 1746 by Bonnie Prince Charlie, to house prisoners taken from General Hawley at Falkirk. Some of these prisoners were ex-students from Edinburgh University. Two of these notable young men, John Home, who was later to find fame as the author of *Douglas*, and Revd J. Wetherspoon, later to become president of Princeton College, plotted their escape and that of four others. They successfully, with the help of knotted bedding, dropped from the kitchen tower and eventually made it back to Edinburgh. The kitchen tower is 17m high and 8m wide – a formidable drop!

*Opposite:* A view of the castle from the Bridge of Teith shows the area of the crossing. This illustrates the strategic importance of the castle and fort and the control exercised over this 'gateway' to the Highlands by the imposing and substantial stronghold. The ferry crossing was said to have been from the old stone stile across to a point about 150yds down the bridge on the south-west side of the Teith. In 1330 this area was called the 'Ville de Doune'. It was in fact part of the Daira Park, the most northerly part of the Blair Drummond Estate. This area was known as the old Cobbilland de Doune from about 1480. A flat-bottomed coble was used until 1535 when the bridge was built. It is thought then that the name Cobbilland came from Coble and it is probable that these boats were made in this area or in an area a mile or so towards Thornhill at a place known as Cobblers Ha.

The massive square tower shown here (centre right), rises to around 80ft above the gateway. The well shown in the centre of the photograph is 20m or so deep. The lord's hall or audience chamber, complete with a musicians gallery, is on the second floor above the gateway, together with the chapel, which lay behind the tiny arched window above the gate passage. The lord's bedroom is on the third level and the other bedrooms on the fourth level. Part of the courtyard seen here is one of the finest in Scotland.

On a lighter note the castle has been used in two well-known films: *Monty Python and the Holy Grail* and *Ivanhoe*. Today the castle is in the care of Historic Scotland on a 999-year lease from the Earl of Moray and is therefore still owned by the Earl. This forward-thinking move will ensure that the castle is maintained over future centuries and will retain its place as a uniquely preserved piece of history. A visit to the castle is essential to fully appreciate its true splendour and magnificent views.

*Opposite:* On the right of the photograph on the second floor is the retainers/great hall, which is 20m long and 8m wide, with a 12m-high ceiling and a central hearth with no actual chimney, just a roof vent. Some of the superb stonework can be seen here and it is hard to think that by the 1800s the castle had fallen into disrepair and was roofless. It was not until the 1880s that the castle was restored by the 14th Earl of Moray. The entrance passage through the tower house is cobbled with an iron outer gate, which is still in position, although the iron inner gate has gone. There is evidence that there may have been a lower outer wall surrounding the castle. (Copyright: Moira Robertson, Deanston)

This view of the castle from the southwest gives a good impression of what the Doune defences would have looked like to the 'visitor' from the south. Slightly further upstream is the shallower water used for one of the crossings. This would have taken the traveller right into the shadow of the castle and, if using the better tracks north, the traveller would have passed right beneath the battlements en route north. The Teith was one of several Scottish rivers noted for fine pearls, often red or pink, but by the end of the nineteenth century pearl fishing was dying out for lack of stock and over-fishing.

DOUNE MILL

# The Doune Castle Mill *(Opposite)*

This lovely illustration shows the picturesque corn mill, which closed in 1939 and dates from before 1528. Andrew Gowans was the last miller who worked in this very traditional mill with its wooden drives, which latterly was leased to Walls of Stirling. The whole area in the vicinity of the castle was probably quite a community, especially in more peaceful times, and it is thought that this site has probably been a settlement of sorts throughout the ages.

The road down to Castle Farm was the original road from Doune to Dunblane passing over the Ardoch at Glenardoch, seen here near the bridge on the left. Nearer the camera is the Glenardoch Coach House. This whole area extending towards the castle is thought to be the original village of Doune and traces of foundations of dwellings can still be seen beside the Ardoch. Later cottages were built on the area above Castle Farm. Glenardoch was known as Doune Cottage; the original cottage was the home of Alexander Ferguson from 1844. During the next twenty years it seems that the house was extended and improved sufficiently for him to host a 'Ball'. Sweetie Sandy, as he was known, was born in a little house in Graham Street. He went on, through his local toffee experiments, to find success eventually in Edinburgh where he 'invented' Edinburgh Rock. With his fortune made, he purchased most of what we now know as Graham Street, which was known as 'Sweetie Lane' before it became Graham Place. Alexander died, aged seventy-three, in Glenardoch in 1871. On the far right of the picture is the Castle Farm House. The well on the immediate right of the picture was called the 'Trootie Well' and was said to be so pure that it was always the home of at least one trout, possibly as a test of contamination. Certainly Peter Morrison, the butcher, was said to take the water for his famous pickles from the well. The Bridge of Ardoch was built in 1735 to replace a wooden bridge called the Bridge of Doune. It is said that Prince Charlie rode over this bridge when visiting Newton in 1745. The new bridge we use today was opened in 1854.

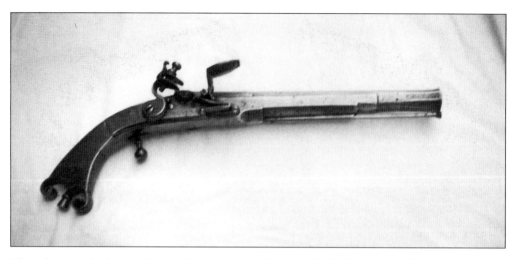

This photograph shows a Doune Pistol made by Thomas Caddell in about 1710. It is believed it was used in the '45 rising and in the American War of Independence. Legend has it that it was a Doune Pistol that fired the first shot – maybe it was this one! It is one of a known 200 Doune Pistols that survive today across the globe. It is well-worn, but the inlaid silver shows evidence of the ornate Celtic oriental design.

Much more detail about the pistol makers of Doune is contained in Archie McKerracher's splendid book *Perthshire in History and Legend*. Martin Kelvin's *The Scottish Pistol* is a very detailed insight into the history, manufacture and design of this sought-after weapon, and includes beautiful plates showing examples of numerous pistols.

This photograph shows the old Burgh town signs, which can be seen in the Kilmadock Development Trust base, at 52 Main Street, Doune. In 1890, the Burgh Crest incorporated the pistols to commemorate their importance. It is sad to see this acknowledgement to Doune's past now dispensed with by the removal of the original signs. Moray S. Mackay designed these town signs and actually made the original wooden signs that can now be seen in the Information Centre.

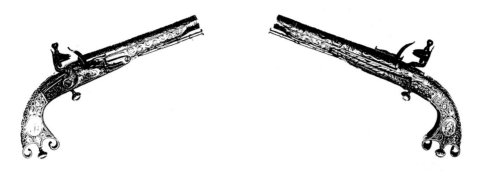

A pair of eighteenth-century gold decorated Scottish all-steel flintock belt pistols by T. Murdoch.

# Doune Pistols

Not only is Doune well-known for its castle but for the locally produced 'Doune Pistol'. During 1646 a seemingly unremarkable blacksmith from Muthil moved to Doune. Thomas Caddell was his name, and he set up business as a gunsmith in what is now known as the Pistol Factory, behind the Old Dairy. It was soon obvious he was a talented and inventive man with a vision for perfection, despite his apparent lack of education. Nothing is known of his early life, which might have given us a better understanding of the man.

He researched the available materials for his trade and came up with a unique process involving the forging of horseshoe nails into a spiral twist. The end product was a highly sought after all-steel pistol, normally highly decorated with Celtic-type designs. As his fame and that of the pistols grew, so did the quality of the finished pistol improve. Many were inlaid with silver and gold and some, made to order, bore the coat of arms of the owner.

This lucrative industry was continued through five generations of Caddells and their apprentices right up until the end of the eighteenth century. Other names that must be given credit here include John Murdoch, whose workshop lay at the corner of Balkerrach Street; the Campbell family workshop was behind the McAlpines Bakery and may have also been used by the Murdoch family. There is also evidence of another workshop in Graham Street and there were probably others including the old gun shop at 53 Main Street. Names such as Christie, Bissett, Sutherland, Paterson, Stuart, Cameron and Mitchie were all known to be accomplished Doune gunsmiths. The old Kilmadock Cemetery by the River Teith contains the graves of a number of these people. Other old blacksmiths' shops within the village are still known as Smiddy, and it is possible that some of these were used to make the odd pistol, given that Doune was a centre for such a lucrative product.

During the eighteenth century much of Main Street, Doune, as we know it today was built, and it is likely that from the late seventeenth century to the end of the eighteenth century Doune owed much of its prosperity to both the Deanston Mill and the Pistol industry. The area was also known for shoemaking and sporran or 'purse' making, no doubt associated with the fact that people with money to spend came to Doune because of the pistols and the Doune fairs, at which leather and hair were readily available.

Recent extensive surveys done over a ten-year period have revealed a great deal of information on the whereabouts of some of the surviving pistols. Understandably, many private owners will be reluctant to declare their wares, so figures are likely to be distorted, but out of 124 pistol makers, 760 Scottish pistols survive and well over a quarter of those were made in Doune. Largely due to the Industrial Revolution and the newly acquired methods of mass productions, the trade for the Doune gunsmiths began to die out. However, the reputation of the highly acclaimed end product has lasted through the ages and these sought-after possessions, which once cost a year's wages, have not lost their relative value.

# *Three*
# Doune Railway Station

The line from Dunblane through Doune to Callander was opened on Monday 28 June 1858 as a single line. It was in mid-February 1857 that the first sod was cut at Cromlix marking the beginning of the Dunblane, Doune & Callander Railway. This was at a time when the magic of the Trossachs was being appreciated by the masses, and the link by coach to Loch Katrine from Callander opened up a considerable amount of trade for all the local communities. It was only a few years earlier that Sir Walter Scott had written *The Lady of the Lake* and sold twenty thousand copies. Such was the developing market for tourists to visit the Trossachs, even locals benefited with a return trip to Stirling for 10*d*!

Doune Railway Station not long after it was opened. It owes much of its grandeur to the fact that the General Manager lived at Inverardoch.

This photograph shows the station when it was first opened, promoting the tourist route to Oban, which was to be one of the most popular scenic routes for the next century.

Doune New Station
(On Tourist Route to Oban.)

Doune Station at the end of the nineteenth century. On the right-hand side you can just make out the privet hedge cut into the shape of a train. When you now drive into Pistolmakers Row, you effectively drive through what was once the station entrance. It is interesting to note that there was a plan to build a line from Stirling to Deanston, Doune and Callander and the prospectus was advertised at the same time as the prospectus for the Dunblane, Doune, Callander line was advertised. It was only the fact that the Scottish Central Railway was about to start building a line from Perth via Dunblane to Stirling that made this the cheapest option.

It was almost forty-four years later that the double-line was opened from Dunblane to Doune, around the time of the opening of the new Doune Station. Considered a top grade station of its day, it may well have had something to do with the fact that Sir James Thompson, who was eventually to become chairman of the Caledonian Railway, resided locally at Inverardoch. The building of the Central Scotland Railway was a tremendous feat of engineering and the navvies or labourers employed could have been forgiven their exuberance at fair time. However it is noted that in 1846 around fifty of them started a battle, which was serious enough to alarm the Burgh for some time afterwards.

In the *Stirling Observer* of 19 February 1857, it was recorded that Doune had a rather busy appearance in the evenings, all due to the amount of work generated by the influx of business caused by the railway. It seems Doune had become a very busy centre and a large amount of indirect but very acceptable trade had resulted. The phrase used to describe the situation was 'that casual disturbances may be expected, and are looked upon as the disagreeable accompaniments of such works'! The same paper talks about the 'annual apology for a market held on the 13th instant as having dwindled into little else than name and the merest shadow of business compared to days gone'. Although still announced with all the pomp of other Scots fairs, it had lost almost all of its former status. It says then that the older inhabitants looked back with sadness at the passing of an era. It is easy to reflect here on the passing of these days being linked to the present day, when our old folk and we ourselves will say it was different in my day, we had more fun, and we mixed more often with our community. Nothing really changes!

A few months later, in May of the same year, it was noted in connection with railway affairs that after the Saturday pay day, breaches of the peace were alarmingly numerous and the town of Doune was in a most disorderly state. It seems that the railway did have a few drawbacks. A hundred and ten years later the line was closed, a very controversial and much debated issue to this day.

Some years later, the station was in less pristine condition, Miss Linda Fox aged nine looks on, witnessing the passing of an era. The last train to London was to pass a few hours later at 8.15 p.m. The railway was closed forever in October 1965.

The bridge over the line which is now part of Campbell's wood yard, where part of the platform can still be made out.

*Left:* Grandpa Jimmy Croy and dog Glen with the east signal box at Doune behind them.

*Right:* Doune Signal Box – 'Home from home' for Chrissie and Lizzy McAlpine relaxing in the tidy homely surroundings of Sammy Blackwood's signal box. Chrissie's husband Simon Ziolkowski was the signalman at the Drumvaich Signal Box.

# *Four*
# The Crofts

## Doune Golf Course

Doune could once boast an excellent nine-hole golf course, which started life in 1903 on an area known locally as 'Wester Hill'. Part of it covered what was to become the sand quarry and later was what we know today as the 'Ponds'. The first pavilion was a temporary affair standing in the low ground near the West Pilings but, through local fundraising, a pavilion was funded and erected, completed about 1905. Further improvements and extensions were implemented over the next twenty years under the driving force of Revd G.S. Mackay. It seems that the demise of the club came with the war years and the advent of the quarry.

The High Hole with the Braes and Uam Var in the far right corner and what was probably the young Black Park and Currachmore Wood behind the dyke.

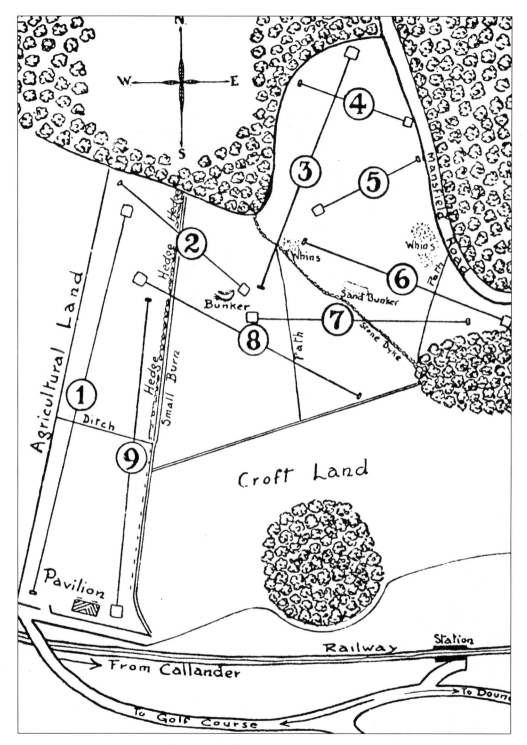

Plan of Doune Golf Course. This rare and interesting plan shows the Croft land that is now the 'Ponds'. It also clearly identifies the round Bluebell Wood above the railway where there was the Cairn, which was eventually revealed to be a burial cist.

DRIVING TO LAST HOLE, DOUNE GOLF COURSE.

The above view shows a slightly different angle from the Nineth Tee. In the background is the Parton Strip (probably derived from 'Parktown Muir') to the west of the Doune-Callander road, with Buchany hidden by the trees. The Buchany Burn was said to have flowed red with blood after a fierce battle between two rival families of Rosehall and Craigton. Tombs found just below Rosehall House may well have been associated with this story. The Parton Strip is a copse or line of trees planted to commemorate the parting of the troops from their loved ones to the ill-fated battle of Flodden around 1513. In the background are the Trossachs and Ben Gullipen above Loch Venachar, and Lennieston Muir.

Our well-dressed golfers show off their splendid golfing attire on the last hole near the pavilion on a lovely summer's day. Behind them is the young Currachmore Wood.

34

Miss Sheila Stroyan and her father, Mr John Stroyan of Lanrick estate, at a golf competition showing the fashionable golfing attire of the day. Miss Stroyan was an accomplished golfer and won the Scottish Girls Championship around 1938.

A scene at Doune Fairs showing the Standing Stone at the Ponds in relation to the probable original location of the Mercat Cross.

Probably a familiar building to many, the Clubhouse (built by MacBeth of Blairdrummond), is now know as Golden Acre and for the best part of the twentieth century has been the home of Isa and John Calder and their children David and Isobel, an accomplished horsewoman. The bike and sidecar dates this picture, it may well have belonged to the Mackay family. The putting green was to the right of the flagpole. This picture was taken in the early part of the nineteenth century in the early days of the course and shows the pond area before the quarry changed the landscape into what we now know as the Ponds.

## Doune Fairs

The area in the above photograph, now thickly wooded, was known as the Crofts, and heavily used during the Doune Fairs. The great roads from Edinburgh to Fort William and from Glasgow to Perth pass through the parish, crossing each other at Doune. Little wonder it became such a thriving community. The area around the Crofts was very open, seen here as a hayfield, but in the years of the Fairs it was let in small sections to villagers for agricultural purposes, like large allotments. The picture also shows the area that was used for the cattle fairs and why it was then so suitable, being mainly flat and dry. The area from the standing stone at the Ponds entrance back to the Black Park and north towards Golden Acre was flat, except for the Bluebell Wood or Round Wood, which was later discovered to be a burial cairn. It was well drained and ideal grazing for such events. Doune Fairs or Trysts were famous throughout Scotland and it is recorded that in the later decade of the eighteenth century some 10,000 head of cattle were sold at the Autumn Fair. A busy place it must have been, and it is easy to visualise the scene. A local poet records the Latter, or early November, fair thus:

> *Into a house you could scarce get a head in*
> *For huxters and drovers and each other loon,*
> *Some were fighting and others courting*
> *Such are the humours of the Fair o'Doune.*

Such a large number of livestock descending on Doune would have been spread over a large area. It is recorded that the Parton Muir, opposite and to the north of Golden Acre, held a village fair from the early seventeenth century. From all accounts the whole area from Carse of

37

Cambus to the Ponds would have been the area of the fairs when the volumes of cattle were in the region of 10,000 head because a considerable area would have been needed. This area would have been well suited being flat with good grazing. How things would have been organised has to be left to the imagination! It seems from all accounts that large-scale organised movement of cattle to such fairs, of which only Falkirk was larger, was possible as the Drove Road system became more orderly. It is said that Doune was as far south as a Highlander would trust his cattle and as far north as a Lowlander or Englishman would trust his gold. It was from the Doune Tryst that Robin Oig set out on the ill-fated journey to England described in Sir Walter Scott's tale *The Two Drovers*!

The fairs evolved over time to be established as:

1. February – For grain and general business.
2. May – For milk cows and cattle.
3. July – The Grosset fair for berries, notably gooseberries, hence the name, also hiring of labour and general business.
4. Early November – The Latter fair, also called the Feein Fair, was a general fair for cattle, sheep, horses and other livestock and hiring of labour and servants.
5. Late November – Martinmas Fair or 'Snawy' Doune for livestock, mainly cattle.
6. Christmas Fair – Tuill Fair for store cattle, grain and general business.

It is natural to understand how the making of sporrans grew in this area at this time, as did the making of shoes, as leather would have always been in plentiful supply. The market in the village was held at the same time and no doubt a great deal of general trading would have been transacted. People from all corners of Scotland would have used this as a real social and business event. Those with a bit more money would have been good customers for the pistol industry and it is perhaps why Thomas Caddell moved here in 1646 to what he may have considered a captive market or at least a very busy place at fair time.

A fair scene – trading pistols.

# *Five*

# Sport

## Football

Doune's football history is a little complicated. Doune Castle Football Club was founded in 1885 and it is mentioned in Peter Baxter's *Football in Perthshire in 1900*. No doubt football of a sort was played in this area for some considerable time before this date. After an intermittent history it was reformed more permanently in 1954. Since then it has maintained a high profile and a number of notable successes include winning the Buchan Trophy in 1963-64, the Loch Trophy in 1960-61, the League Division One in 1961-62, the Robertson Trophy in 1975-76, the Campbell Trophy in 1983-84, the Scottish Brewers in 1985-86, and the League Division Two in the same season. In 1970 they played in the Scottish Cup finals at Hampden.

The Vale of Teith football team was founded in 1877 and was known to play on the park around Tullochan Knowe, a very prominent little hill which may be a burial cairn. Tullochan Knowe is situated on Ashmill Road, the 'back Callander road from Deanston'. It appears that Burn Murdoch from Gartincaber allowed the club to use his land. In 1877, when the Vale joined the Scottish Football Association, it was noted as holding supremacy over Callander and Dunblane. It had thirty members and the colours were blue and white. By 1884 they had fifty members and won more games than they lost.

When the Perthshire Football Association was formed, Doune was able to produce two teams such was the population of the district, influenced heavily by the mill workers. These teams were Vale of Teith and Teith Bank Rovers. In 1881 the Vale was recorded as a noteworthy club capable of playing a major team with a first and a second eleven, but it seems to have disappeared around 1894. However the Teith Bank Rovers were revived as a junior club around 1899. Mention of successful games played between the 'Vale' men and the Dunblane 'Wanderers' (also referred to as the Cathedral leather hunters) are recorded in that year's paper of 15 October 1881. They are referred to as Kilmadockians who had pluck, stamina and staying power in the ferocity of a fast and coarse game!

The *Observer* records, in 1883, the observations of a disgruntled 'supporter' who came to watch the club play against the formidable King's Park team. He did not feel he had his money's worth and complained it cost 3d for entrance and the game only lasted an hour, partly in the dark, and was rubbish. He also comments that his 3d was used to subsidise a good feed in the Woodside afterwards. It is interesting to note that this area was also known for quoit playing from 1894 to 1904. Quoiting was also played in Doune on land on the Argaty road just past the railway bridge.

Doune Castle Football Club, winners of Perthshire Consolation Cup 1908-1909. From left to right, back row: G. Anderson, J. Cardy. Middle row: D. Henderson, J. M'Leod, W. M'Kellar, J. Scott, A. McAnish (secretary), S. Hastie, A. Sloan, T. Tunnah, D. M'Duff (treasurer) J. Forbes (team manager). Front row: R. James, R. Yound, J. Millar, J. Morrison (captain), R. MacFarlane, A. Collier, J. Law. Photograph taken in the Moray Park, Doune. James Forbes, the team manager, was chosen in his younger days to play in the Scotland Junior team and he also played in the army team during the First World War.

1964-1965, Doune Castle, Amateur Football Club League Championship and Buchan Trophy Winners, Stirling & District Amateur Football Association. From left to right, back row: J. Bisset, D. McTurk, S. McIntosh, E. McLean, J. Cunningham, E. McKie, E. Dow, M. Watson, W. Docherty, P. Thompson. Front row: E. Hammill, R. Scott, W. Rankin, S. Thompson, W. Cowie, H. Mailer. (Copyright: Whyler Photos, Stirling)

*Opposite*: Deanston Footbell Club, 1960s. Back row, from left to right: Tiger Shaw (trainer), Neil McDougal, Billy Cameron, Alex McFarlane, Hugh Reid, -?-, Jack Matheson, Billy Kenny (manager). Front row: Jackie Knowles, George Carson, Billy Miller, Robert Matheson, George Wilson.

# Bowling

Doune Castle Bowling Club is thought now to be the third oldest surviving club in Scotland. The first formal green was on the ground to the rear of the Star Inn, today known as the Mile End, which has been the home of Harvey Maps for many years. A newspaper cutting from the *Stirling Journal and Advertiser* dated 25 May 1860 says that Mr Gray, the then proprietor, generously funded this expensive enterprise. So those first bowlers were in fact playing in the area of the Roman Fort and never knew it!

The second formal home of the club was in an area known as Potters Field. This green in Balkerach Street was opened on Friday 28 July 1876.

The club's popularity grew with an ever increasing membership. A three-year funding programme resulted in the club moving to its final resting place in 1925 at great expense, spending £274 12s 3d on laying a new green. The club seems to have always been successful, with the usual ups and downs of committee life! In 1975 the land was purchased from the Moray estates for £1,000, and in 1981 the new clubhouse was opened, with the function suite opening in 1985. A proactive club, by pooling its expertise and resources achieved a much admired and envied facility of which they should be very proud. The present clubhouse is full of the evidence of a long and successful life with trophies, cups and photographs galore. Today the club continues its success with an established successful junior team.

In the summer of 1876 the green relocated to what was then known as the Potter's field, an area of land at the west end of the village opposite Woodside Cottage, which is now the home of Mr and Mrs J. Blackwood. A formal photograph in front of the Clubhouse, from around that time, sporting the West Perthshire Bowling League cup around 1915.

Tending the green at the Potters field – a working evening on the green taken around 1922. In the background on the right are the station sheds. This area is now the site of the modern bungalows in Balkerach Street, next to the stationmaster's house.

The opening of the new clubhouse in 1981, with its modern facilities representing a real achievement. Most of the hard physical work was done by members and friends.
From left to right, front row kneeling: -?-, Willie Stewart, Ella McAnish, Shawny Donald, John Meeks, Bruce Rawding, Sammy Craig. Second row: Robert Palmer, Jack McLeod, Jim 'Tiger Shaw', -?-, Jack Duff, Noni Palmer, -?-, Hilda Armstrong, Bill Kenny, Lizzy Cameron.

Opening of the new green at Northlea on Saturday 14 May 1927 beside the Rural Hall. Capt. A.S. Mackay declared the green and pavilion open, recalling some of the Club's early days, including a very keen game which ended in the dark and resulted in a pair of bowls being lost for over a week! He made mention of some of the clubs successes: the Templeton Trophy, the M'Intyre Trophy and the Perthshire Trophy. He noted that the game of bowls was for those who had passed the age where more violent games had charms! He felt that this was not accurate in his opinion, having observed 'the violence of gesticulation and the weird forms of physical exercise that some members went through in the course of a game'. Mrs Mackay threw the first jack and was presented with a silver jack on a stand. Photographs of the ceremony were taken by Mr Muir of Callander and were on view for sale at the sum of 4d each.

The first club match to be played on the new green, against Dunblane bowling club, took place on 21 May 1927 – the results were Doune Castle 69 and Dunblane 77. The Commemoration cup was played for on that day. The final was between Club President Mr W. Graham and Mr James McAlpine, whose scores were 9 and 21 respectively.

Back row, from left to right: -?-, -?-, -?-, Murray (coalman), -?-, Bob McAlpine, -?-, -?-, William Able, -?-, -?-, -?-, -?-, -?-, -?-, -?-, Captain A.S. Mackay, -?-, Mrs Mackay, Mackay, -?-, Kev Hockay, Graham the grocer, -?-, -?-, -?-, David Pearson, Tom Corrie (editor of the *Observer*), Jimmy Croy, -?-, -?-, John McIntosh, Jimmy Balfour, -?-.
Front row, from left to right: -?-, -?-, Pete the Post, -?-, Brown, -?-, J. McAlpine, -?-, -?-, -?-, Mr J. McAnish, -?-, Sandy Neil, -?-, -?-, -?-, -?-, William McAnish.

# Curling

Doune Curling Club was founded in 1732, and is recorded as the second oldest club in the world. From 1843 it was a member of the Royal Caledonian Curling Club which was founded around 1830, and in 1935 it was one of 735 clubs worldwide from China to Nova Scotia, of those some 489 were in Scotland! It is interesting to note that in that year there were eighteen regular members and fifteen occasional members, and the Earl of Moray was the President. In 1874 at the Grand Match at Carsebreck, Doune had the highest club score on the losing side.

A somewhat dubious rumour hints at Loch Mahaick being the home of ancient curling in Scotland, who knows! In those early years they used the pond alongside the Lundie Burn just below the Westerton Farm at the top of the Commonty walk. Then, it was very much the sport of the aristocrats and the wealthy and often workers would be called upon to play for the princely sum of 6d a day!

The unusual Points Trophy, made from a cow horn decorated with silver. It may well have been used for occasional matches years ago in the days of hard winters.

The last curling pond was opened by the Earl of Moray in 1903 but was never wholly successful as it was spring fed and spring water does not readily freeze. This pond was in the area off the main A84 opposite the entrance to the Wood of Doune on the right-hand-side travelling north. Although the pond is no longer used and has been planted over by the estate, the club still survives and like many of its type, uses local rinks for competition and recreational play. The last Grand Match was on the Lake of Menteith in 1979.

On 21 January 2001 members and friends of Doune Curling Club had what is believed to be their first outdoor mini 'Bonspiel' to be held on Doune Ponds.

Curling on the Westerton Pond c.1900, Doune v. Blair Drummond and Thornhill. One story associated with this ancient curling pond is that, during the winter of 1745-1746, the curlers were marching up to the ice when they were challenged by a detachment of Prince Charlie's army who mistook their brooms for muskets!

# Cricket

Peter Culbert, who worked at the Cotton Mill, formally established Doune Castle Cricket Club in 1886. Although they thought they had acquired a piece of ground on which to play, difficulties arose and they soon found themselves homeless. So it seems have been the ups and down of cricket in this area. The club went into hibernation every few years, the longest period being thirty-eight years between 1912 and 1950. In the early days they played anywhere and everywhere and it is said on one such occasion they inevitably found themselves batting balls in unacceptable directions! They hit the Earl of Moray's coach, a lucky shot indeed for when the Earl learned of their plight he granted the club the use of what we now know as the Moray Park. The first game was played there on 12 June 1888 against a team raised by Sir John Muir. The players are said to have worn straw hats, flannel jackets and white shirts with white bow ties. In 1955 the club seemed to find stability when it became a member of the Central Cricket league. In those days the talented Davie Murdoch and Ian Bain took the club to some respectable successes. Cousins John and Ian Bain were primarily responsible for holding the club together for some twenty years. The Mailer, Campbell and Murdoch families all played a part in keeping the club going. In common with many clubs, home games enjoyed the hospitality of the cricket wives who were always able to put on a formidable spread. Things improved still further in the 1990s with a lot of support from an active committee and generous support from the Highland Hotel. The youngsters at the primary schools are all introduced to cricket and have given some very impressive performances.

Doune Cricket Club – 1961 Campbeltown. From left to right, back row: Sandy Bryce, David Brown, Sandy McIntosh, Ian Mailer, John Gamble, Tom Campbell, Hamish Mailer. Front row: Billy Jamieson, Ian Bain, Mr Muckersie, John Bain, Bobby Campbell.

Ian Bain holding the Forth Valley Cricket League Cup – won by Doune Cricket Club, 11 September 1964. Ian was also the last Provost of Doune before regionalisation in 1975. Ian, a well-respected businessman, a real family man and true cricketer, died in 2000.

## Angling

As long as people have lived alongside the river, the Teith has been fished either for sport, pleasure, food or a combination of all three. A formal club was formed at a meeting in the Woodside Hotel on 25 April 1876. Most club activities in those days were competition fishing and regular fishing of the Teith was not permitted apart for competitions. The club these days has to apply strict limits on membership, allowing only those people who live within 1km of the Cross to become members. Generally, the club is allowed to fish the River Teith and the Ardoch on two days a week for sea trout and salmon, and brown trout for six days. Many tales are told of adventures on the water including 'blazing the Teith', which involved spearing salmon by torchlight. Using a pickaxe, during the winter of 1894 was unusual but effective. A sport said to take place on Loch Mahaick was using geese to catch pike by tying a baited line to the bird's foot, then driving it out over the water. Once a catch was made, the bird instinctively came to land, exhausted and bringing with it the somewhat surprised pike!

# Six
# The Military

This photograph shows Lt J.M. Morrison, whose family had a sweet shop business on Main Street. Alongside is the Christmas card he sent to John and Isa Calder. Unfortunately, a short time after this he was killed in action. This is a poignant reminder of the fragility of life. Jack, like others in our community and those around the country, was just one young man willing to sacrifice his life for his country.

*Above:* The Morrison 'sweetie' shop in relation to the Balhaldie where Sandy Stewart would probably have been the publican at the time. The Balhaldie, meaning place or steading of the Hazel, dates officially from 1732, but in fact is probably much older.

*Left:* This is thought to be Jack Morrison outside his parent's shop in Main Street. People still remember the sweetie shop, which they used to race to after school. It was run by Mrs Morrison after her husband died in the First World War and then run by her daughter Cathy.

*Right:* Taken c.1914. From left to right: Harry McKenzie, Martha MacKenzie and Danny MacKenzie. An anxious but proud mother hopes the war will soon be over and for her sons safe return.

*Below:* 6/7 Black Watch inter-company football championship, 1922 winners – No.2 Company. From left to right, back row: CQMS McCabe, Lt Cpl Jack, Pte Davidson, Pte Docherty, Pte Paton, Sgt Cramb, CSM Hooks. Middle row: Lt Cpl Campbell, Lt Cpl Camerson, Pte Kennedy, Capt. J.L. Pullar, Pte Connelly, Cpl Jack, Pte Strang.
Front: Cpl MacDonald.

Here is a very mature and brave sixteen-year-old, off to join his regiment, the Scottish Horse Duke of Atholl clan, in 1937. Like many others locally he left home at an early age to face the unknown perils of war. Henry MacKenzie, from 47/49 Balkerach Street (The Gebelman Barbers business), was one of eight children, and was to transfer to the Royal Engineers in 1939. He was later to be mentioned in dispatches for distinguished and gallant service.

By the KING'S Order the name of
*Sapper H. W. Mackenzie,*
*Royal Engineers,*
was published in the London Gazette on
*10 September, 1943,*
as mentioned in a Despatch for distinguished service.
I am charged to record
His Majesty's high appreciation.

Secretary of State for War

A copy of the King's appreciation for Henry Mackenzie's distinguished service.

Sir James and Lady Thompson presented the memorial fountain in Doune, to the Burgh in July 1903, in memory of their daughter Edith. The date of this event was the anniversary of her birth. The family moved to Inverardoch in 1898 when Sir James was General Manager for the Caledonian Railway. When he died in 1906 he had become chairman of this all-important network. The fountain bears the inscription: 'I was thirsty and you gave me drink'. The land was donated by the United Free Church and the work undertaken by James Innes, under the supervision of Mr Christie and W. Gibson, the road surveyor. The fountain itself is constructed of Peterhead granite and was made by Bower & Florence, the Spittal Granite Works, Aberdeen. It was also hoped that the fountain would never run dry as long as the town of Doune existed. The fountain is now dry and planted with flowers, and Doune still flourishes. How things have changed! This photograph shows a large gathering of villagers and visitors among whom are: Miss Louise Campbell of Inverardoch, Misses Murray Menzies, Mrs Mackay, Dr & Mrs Andrew, James B. Macindoe, Chas Gardiner and Mrs Gardiner from Tower of Lethendy, Capt. Jarvis Gregory and Mrs Gregory, Dunblane, Revd Peat, Bailie Forbes, Provost Revd G.S. Mackay presided. Mr Macindoe had been asked to standing in for Sir James Thompson who was unable to attend because of commitments in 'Homburg'.

A makeshift war memorial in the Cross area *c.*1919. In the First World War sixty-three men belonging to the parish died. Their names are listed below. It seems nearly every family in the community was torn apart by this war. Eventually the war memorial took its place to stand as a permanent reminder and was dedicated in July 1922. This very emotional ceremony was presided over by Dr Burn Murdoch of Gartincaber and the memorial was unveiled by Sir Ian Hamilton. Even the schoolchildren left posies of flowers around the monument. We owe them so much that what we must never do is forget them. The names below are shown as they appear on the memorial.

**Royal Navy**
SWO Stuart Hay Murray

**Royal Field Artillery**
Private James Rorie

**Royal Garrison Artillery**
Major Lindsay Bruce Stark Christie

**Royal Engineers**
Sapper Matthew Connelly

**The Cameronians (Scottish Rifles)**
Private James Dick
Private Charles Mills

**The Royal Scots**
Lieutenant William Maxwell Robertson
Corporal Robert Winter

Private John Dickie

**The Royal Scots Fusiliers**
Lieutenant William Cochrane

**King's Own Scottish Borderers**
Private James Allan

**Loyal North Lancashire Regiment**
Private Alexander Duncan

**The Highland Light Infantry**
Private William Watt Shields

**Seaforth Highlanders**
Captain Arthur Buchanan Baillie Hamilton
Private Thomas Rorie
Private Morten Winter

## The Queen's Own Cameron Highlanders
Corporal John Mackay
Private David Black
Private Alexander Cameron
Private Walter Martin
Private Donald M'Callum

## Argyll & Sutherland Highlanders
Lance Corporal Stephen Hastie
Private John Davie
Private Roderick Mackenzie

## Indian Army 20th DCO (Brownlow's Punjabis)
Captain Colin Thomas Burn-Murdoch

## Canadian Expeditionary Force
Private John Paterson Cameron
Private William Downie Maclaren
Private Charles Murray

## The Gordon Highalnders
Private Robert Blennie
Private John Robertson

## Scots Guards
Private William M'Leod
Private Robert Osborne
Private John Piggot

## The Black Watch
(Royal Highland Regiment)
Sergeant James Bell Jackson
Sergeant Michael Manning

Corporal John Blacklock
Corporal Peter Campbell
Lance Corporal Patrick Fallon
Lance Corporal Peter Innes
Lance Corporal Duncan M'Coll
Lance Corporal John M'Gregor
Lance Corporal George Reilly
Private James Blacklock
Private William Boyd
Private Andrew Campbell
Private David Campbell
Private Alexander Dingwall
Private James Galbraith
Private John Graham
Private John Hislop
Private Robert Holmes
Private James Liles
Private George Marshall
Private James Marshall
Private Archibald Miller
Private William Miller
Private John Moffat
Private Malcolm M'Donald
Private Daniel M'Naughton
Private Robert M'Naughton
Private David M'Vey
Private James Salmond
Private James Stewart

## The Inscription

TO THE GLORY OF GOD AND MEMORY OF THE MEN OF THE PARISH OF KILMADOCK WHO GAVE THEIR LIVES FOR KING AND COUNTRY IN THE GREAT WAR 1914-1919.
See ye to it that these shall not have died in vain.

On the side of the old Mill at Deanston, which is now the Distillery, is a plaque as a memorial to the following who gave their lives in the Great War, 1914-1918. Some names are also included above.

John Piggott, Alexander Mackay, John Graham, Duncan Walker, James Blacklock, Peter Campbell, George Reilly, David Campbell, John Dickie, John Hislop, James Moffat, Daniel McNaughton, John Moffat, John Blacklock, James Clark, Charles Gardner, Arthur Warren, Henry Liddell, Alexander Duncan, Alexander Cameron, James Allan, James Rorie, Robert Walker, Thomas Rorie, Alexander Stewart, Stuart Hay Murray, Thomas Rorie Jnr., James Stewart, James Jackson, William Moffat, James Moffat.

The War Memorial being unveiled at a service on 3 August 1922 by General Sir Ian Hamilton. The Hall was a gift to the Burgh from Sir A.K. Muir of Blair Drummond and, after it was completed in 1922, was used as the Council Offices and the Surveyor's office. In the Second World War, eighteen men from the area lost their lives. Doune, however, was never bombed during this war. It is interesting to note that much debate took place about whether the village should have a public hall or a memorial. This controversial issue was resolved when Sir A.K. Muir made the generous offer to provide a hall. The Earl of Moray presented the committee with the site for the memorial on the edge at the ancient Wood of Doune. The memorial is made of Auchenheath stone from a quarry in Lanarkshire, the same stone that was used for the hall. Both the hall and the war memorial were opened within a week of each other.

Those of the Second World War who are remembered on the memorial, include:

**Royal Army Ordnance Corps**
Private T. Bain
Private D.K. Dewar

**Coldstream Guards**
Lieutenant H.C.H. Bowser

**Royal Air Force**
Pilot Officer I. Brodie
Sergeant Pilot S.D. Cameron
Flight Lieutenant W. Hamilton

**National Fire Service**
Captain I. Campbell

**Cameron Highlanders**
Corporal D. Cormack

**Blackwatch** (RHR)
Private D. Don

**Royal Navy**
AB R. Drummond

**Argyll & Sutherland Highlanders**
Private J. Hunter
Private G. Dalgleish

**Royal Artillery**
Gunner T. McLeod
Lieutenant C.C. Orr

**46th Reconnaisance Regiment**
Lieutenant J.M. Morrison

**King's Own Scottish Borderers**
Corporal D.M. Reid

**Scots Rifles**
Rifleman D. Wilson

**Royal Engineers**
Sapper C. Young

At Deanston, on the old Mill (now the distillery)r, the following are also remembered:
John Hunter, David Don, David Wilson, Thomas McLeod, Donald Cormack.

'D' COMPANY.     5th BN. PERTHSHIRE HOME GUARD.

Sitting (left to right)—Lieut. G. A. Buchan,   Lieut. H. W. Chisholm,   Lieut. J. McQueen,   Major A. M. McGrigor,   Lieut.-Col. P. D. Stirling. O.B.E., M.C.,
O.C. 3 Pln.                   O.C. 5 Pln.                 O.C. 4 Pln.            2 i/o 5 Perth Bn.              Commanding 5 Perth Bn.
Major D. C. Bowser, O.B.E.,   Capt. I. G. Charleson,   Lieut. J. Cramb,   Lieut. S. G. Corbishley.
O.C. 'D' Coy.       2 i/o 'D' Coy., O.C. 1 Pln.   O.C. 6 Pln.       O.C. 2 Pln.
Standing (left to right)—Lieut. D. Crombie,   Lieut. G. Rawding,   Capt. R. Macfarlane,   2/Lieut. R. Rattray,   Capt. R. Bruce, K.O.S.B.,   2/Lieut. T. Macfarlane,
3 Pln.                   5 Pln.               M.O. 'D' Coy.         4 Pln.               Adjt. 5 Perth Bn.             4 Pln.
Lieut. G. K. Moffat,   Lieut. E. G.Gardiner,   Lieut. J. Lindsay Pullar, O.B.E.,   Lieut. A. Broadfoot,   Lieut. J. Caul.   Lieut. W. G. Taylor.
A.O. 1 & 6 Plns.         3 Pln.               H.Q. A.O.                   1 Pln.               2 Pln.           1 Pln.
(Absent—2/Lieut. Ballantyne.)

Star Photos. Perth.

Home Guard at Argaty, pictured outside the main entrance door.

# Seven

# Religious Life

The original site of the old Kilmadock Church. This was the first Presbyterian Church in the area, at the site of the old cemetery beside the Teith at the confluence of the Annat Burn, and dates back to around 1560. Wherever there is an Annat there are traces of an ancient chapel or cemetery. The word is often associated with a fine well or clear stream. This church operated until 1743 when it moved to Doune. The buildings were pulled down and some of the stone was used in the new Kilmadock church. Both this early church and the present church were built on the triangle of land between Moray Street and King Street on Main Street. This picture, taken around 1945, shows the cemetery and the partial remains of the Kilmadock Church, where the Annat Burn meets the Teith river. This is a very important site and it is widely thought that, when, in the seventh century, St Cadoc travelled from Ireland, his followers established a series of churches in the Vale of Menteith in Kilmadock parish. The seven chapels associated with Kilmadock are: Annat, Lanrick, Torrie, Walton, Bridge of Teith (Christ's Well), Newton and St Fillans's within the Castle. The parish name of Kilmadock translates as 'Church of my Doc', or loosely translated 'Doig's Church'. The ancient family of 'Dog' have long had associations with Kilmadock and Doune. This old kirk yard shows grave marks of the Dogs of Menteith and it is known to include line drawings of stones that date back to 1618. It probably holds secrets of a much earlier time that one day will be revealed.

The McIntosh girls, Sarah, Barbara and Daisy, enjoy a summer's afternoon with mother Janet and Nipper the dog. The track on the right of the picture is the route that went from Kilmadock to Buchany and latterly, after the railway was built, from Kilmadock to Burn of Cambus up the Annat glen.

This whole site is immensely important as it is believed to have been one of the early sites of Christianity in Scotland. The area on which young Jimmy McIntosh is sitting in 1932 was known locally as the Hanging Area and it has long been thought to be the original site of the first Culdees monastry, dating back to c.600 AD. An area of stones formed an oval shape, maybe 30ft by 60ft in size, but the stones are now cleared away to the banks of the Teith where evidence can still be seen of an unusual volume of shaped stones. No doubt one day this area will be excavated and it will give up its secrets. Old Kilmadock houses and manse can be seen through the long grass: a real community in those days.

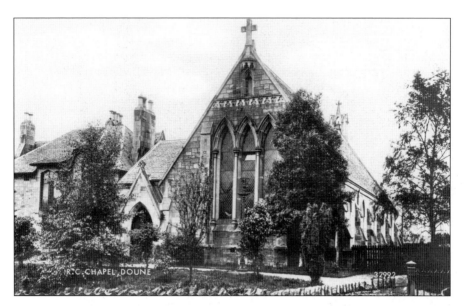

*Above:* The Catholic Church was built in 1875 and holds about 300 people. Mrs Campbell of Inverardoch was heavily involved in the plans for the establishment of the church. Before this, Catholics in Doune were said to walk to Stirling barefoot regardless of the weather, with their boots carried around the neck, and to put them on only before entering the town and the church in Stirling. The house on the left was demolished in the early 1960s.

*Opposite:* The first East Church, as the Kilmadock Church became known, was finally completed around 1746. Services had been held in the castle during the intervening years. It is likely it stood back from the road originally, as there was no cemetery attached to it. The old cemetery at Old Kilmadock was in use right up until the mid-twentieth century. Between 1820 and 1824 the completely new church that we know today was built to seat 1,000. Here it is seen in Doune around 1900 still with spires and railings and the clock with its black face. This clock was replaced for the more common white face around 1930 by Briggs & Ferrier and eventually made electric in 1970. The splendid arms of the Earl of Moray are still intact today and can be seen above the main entrance archway. Minor internal improvements, made over the years, are all that changed during the intervening century. This was the established church in the parish until the Union of Churches in 1929.

One story that lingers on concerns an incident in the 1950s when, during a thunderstorm, the local bus which was being watched by Roy Doy, turned out from King Street and was narrowly missed being flattened by one of the spires, which had been hit by lightening. All the spires were removed after this incident.

The house nearest the church was owned by Campbell the shoemaker, and you can see the double doors, which have now vanished. The Balhaldie Inn, which can be seen in the background before it was extended, dates from 1732, but it is likely that there was a similar watering hole in this location long before that time.

The West Church, built in 1867 by the congregation of the Kilmadock Free Church, seated 800. The hall was added in 1890 and it finally became the Drill Hall when the Perthshire Volunteers took it over in 1868. The original church was a low building with little by way of comforts. The union with the United Presbyterian Church in 1900 meant that the Free Church became the United Free Church and, with the union with the Established Church in 1929, the name changed to the Kilmadock West Church.

In 1961, the church was purchased by James Innes & Son and was converted to a very tasteful residence. The spire was also removed about this time.

The Scottish Episcopal Church of St Medoc's a smaller church holding about 120, was built some three years later in 1878. Services prior to this were held in a small building in Graham Street, which had its own manse accessible by a carriageway from George Street just opposite Bank Street. This was all removed when the present Rosebank House was enclosed with a high stone wall. Interestingly, this early building was constructed on two levels with an open wall allowing the clergy to minister to twice the prescribed number of parishoners allowed at that time.

The Christian Brethren have the Gospel Hall in Balkerach Street, which still exists to this day.

The Wesleyan Chapel in George Street was built in 1844 at the corner of Bank Street; eventually this was converted to a house.

The Auld Licht Church in Graham Street was built in 1801 by the congregation of the Brig o' Teith Church. For some years they had no real base and often conducted services in the open. After a period of disruption and change they effected a union with the church in Graham Street and it was then known as the Deanston Church, then the Free Church of Doune until finally in 1871 the church closed. The premises in George Street are now converted into houses. It is remarkable to note that one of the church ministers was happy to walk to Doune from Stirling to conduct his services and return to Stirling on foot at night!

*Above:* The Bridge of Teith Church stood in the area of an ancient chapel. It is possible that this is the site of one of the seven chapels of Kilmadock – Christ's Well. Indeed a well was discovered between the back door of the church and riverbank. It is also thought that stones relating to the old chapel are incorporated into the south-west part of the bridge. This area was quarried for the making of the bridge, which was built in 1535. Eventually the Congregation of Menteith built its church on the site in 1743. In 1832, the last church on this site was built with the manse following in 1833. In 1929, after its union with the Relief Church in 1847 as the United Presbyterian Church, it joined with the Established Church to become the Church of Scotland, turning back history 200 years! In 1948 the Bridge of Teith Church closed and the congregation and funds passed to the East and West Churches in Doune, and Deanston Mill took over the site. The church was eventually demolished in the early 1960s.

The first Independent or Congregational Church was on the site of the Moray Institute, and traces its routes back to the Chaplains of Cromwell. The church was dissolved in 1858/1859 and was then used as the Parochial Board Room and reading room. This was the base for the Town Council when Doune became a Police Burgh in 1890 and a base for the Burgh offices until the Muir Hall was built in 1922.

*Above:* This chapel stands on the banks of the Ardoch and dates from 1864. Saint Bridgid or Brite is commemorated here. Kilbryde is not thought to be one of the ancient Chapels of Kilmadock but lies very near to the site of an old 'Roman' Bridge. Nearby lie two huge conglomerate stones; one of which was originally brought down to its final resting place, at the end of the ice age, from the Callander area. On the opposite side of the Ardoch is Kilbryde Castle, which was built around 1460 and has been the home of the Campbells since 1643. During the time of the previous owners, the Grahams, the castle was once thought to be haunted by Lady Anne Chisholm who was murdered as a result of an unsuccessful love affair. Her body was finally discovered through her ghostly wanderings and laid to rest in her family graveyard at Cromlix.

Another local character lived on the moors above Kilbryde. Heather Jock, who was politely described as a weaver and dog breeder, was known more commonly as a thief and poacher with a deadly shot that no one dared to cross. The remains of his 'bit hoosie' in the Glen or Smuggler Road, as it was sometimes called, can still just be seen. He was born in a thatched cottage in the grounds of Old Newton. Eventually his past caught up with him and he was transported to Botany Bay in Australia along with a few hundred other convicts.

The Moray Institute had a library, a reading room and a billiard table, something referred to as far back as 1898! Like the Moray Park, the Institute was a gift to the village from the Earl of Moray. This picture shows the famous billiard table in the Institute around 1922, with Sam Blackwood in action in the foreground. From left to right behind are Bobby Connelly, Duncan Bruce, Ian Bruce and Peter Connelly. It is said that they got such a fire going they could only play at one end of the table!

A charter dated 2 November 1789 established the St James's Lodge of Doune Freemasons, No.171. In 1815 they eventually managed to build their own hall, the Union Hall. The opening of this hall was celebrated by a torchlight musical procession to the three bridges of Doune. Drinking a toast around the Cross followed this celebration. The lodge has survived some difficult times and still thrives to this day.

# *Eight*
# The Estates

**Inverardoch**
The splendid façade of Inverardoch House, built in 1859, sat as the name suggests, on the high ground overlooking the mouth of the Ardoch where it meets the Teith below the castle. The house was severely damaged by fire just twenty years after it was built, but had been restored as of the date of this later photograph. During the early years of the railway, between 1898 and 1902, the General Manager of the railway and his wife, Sir James and Lady Thompson, lived in the house. Sir James was also Chairman of the Caledonian Railway. This inevitably gave the station an important status! It was used by the military during the war and, as a result, was left in need of costly remedial work. A number of Norwegian and Polish soldiers were stationed here for a time during the Second World War. Some were to marry local lasses and settle in the area. In 1951 the house was stripped of its roof and left to the elements until it was finally flattened. Inverardoch Chapel stands just a short walk downstream on the banks of the Teith. It is one of seven associated with the Old Kilmadock monastery, it was known as the Chapel of Newton or St Fillan's without the Castle.

**Row**

The Fogo family taken outside the 'new house' in 1861. Roughly translated, 'Row' means a promontory or point of land sticking into the sea; the estate and house stand on the side of the Teith on the old sea margins. It is thought that the site has been a settlement since ancient times and the present house, which was built in 1850, was built a little distance from the original house. This was home of the Fogo family between 1596 and 1969. The family originated from Lorraine in France, but moved north to Row from the Scottish borders in the late sixteenth century.

## Old Newton (*opposite*)

Old Newton is known as the oldest surviving building in the area. It has strong connections with the Keepers of Doune Castle and it may have been connected to the castle by some underground passage. It is recorded that Prince Charlie halted his horse here in 1745 on his way south to the Ford at Frew. He took a glass of wine offered to him by the attractive Miss Edmonstone who asked to kiss his hand. Her wish was duly granted! This rash act prompted a young cousin, Miss Clemintina, to ask for a kiss on the lips, not an easy task as the Prince never dismounted from his horse! Sir Walter Scott also stayed here and it is thought that he wrote some of *The Lady of the Lake* when he stayed in the house.

## Blair Drummond

On the south banks of the Teith lies the Blair Drummond estate. Central to the old estate was the impressive Blair Drummond House, built around 1870. It took the place of the original old house, which was built around 1716 by George Drummond. It was owned by George Stirling Home-Drummond-Moray at the time of this photograph. The original entrance to the 'long avenue' to the estate was from the lodge at the Ashmill Burn. This was re-routed as a result of a bad carriage accident down the steep slope when, in 1852, the Chain Lodge was built, just a few hundred yards over the Bridge of Teith on the left side of the A84.

Sir A.K. Muir, eldest son of Sir John Muir of Deanston, bought the estate in 1913, and having no children, he left the estate to his nephew Sir John Muir. Around 1923 the house was altered after a bad fire. The Safari Park was opened in the 1970s, and today is owned and run by Jamie Muir. The house was re-named Camphill when it was taken over by the Camphill Blairdrummond Trust. It is run as a community for young adults, sixteen to twenty-five years old, with special needs.

BLAIR DRUMMOND HOUSE, DOUNE                                    31754

Blair Drummond cannot be mentioned without a reference to Lord Kames, described as an inventive genius. Much of the estate was changed from bleak barren waste to a Scottish Garden of Eden. He was responsible for the organised clearance of the Kincardine Moss using various methods dependent on the depth and quality of the moss. Between 1770 and 1799 around 280 acres were reclaimed and they supported 126 families. During this clearance a Roman causeway was discovered running south-east to north-west. The moss was between 8ft and 14ft thick and the most successful and innovative method of removal was digging by hand and flotation by water through man-made canals into the Rivers Teith and Forth. Water taken by Persian wheel, which carried 160 buckets from the Teith, was conveyed by pipe and aqueduct on to the moss. In 1774 the moss extended to some 1,800 acres of which 1,500 belonged to Lord Kames. Hence with deep ploughing and draining the moss was turned slowly into a fertile plain that was highly productive.

The moss clearances warrant their own book; it is such a complex and interesting story. The following publications recall the history of this tremendous feat: Stuart J. McCulloch *Fawn Hill and its Environs*; Archie McKerracher *Perthshire in History and Legend*.

## Argaty

Argaty as it was before alterations to the front door and the tower, pre-1926. The tree on the left was known as the 'Rabbits' Parlour'. Roughly translated Argaty means 'windy heights'. Back in 1497, after being forfeited to the crown by James the First when the Duke of Albany was executed at Stirling, Argaty was gifted to Sir Patrick Home; so started some 400 or so years of occupation by the Homes. The estate was much larger in the early days and the original house much grander, but now the only part of it which remains is the kitchen and rear access area. The Home family had associations with Argaty since the sixteenth century. It is interesting to note that in those days there were numerous obligations on tenants to provide the estate with certain goods. Each tenant was ordained to plant six barren trees within their enclosures. The laird provided the trees, while all manure had to be applied to the land under penalty of ten pounds! In the mid-nineteenth century the estate gained a name for shorthorn cattle under the lairdsmanship of George Home Monro Binning Home. He was considered a good laird and died in 1884. Some thirty-three years or so later, in 1917, the estate was sold, so ending the dynasty of the Homes of Argaty and its 'Kings Lundies'. It is thought that much of the reduction in the size of the estate was due to the 'support' given by the estate to the cause of Charles the First. The associations with William Binning of Wallyford and David Monro account for the story behind the carved stone on a gable over the round tower of the house, which shows a shield with a wagon on it. One of Binning's relatives was involved in the capture of Linlithgow Castle. In 1308 he drove a cart of hay under the portcullis, thereby allowing his seven sons to attack the guard and allowing the capture of the castle to take place.

Mr and Mrs Henderson bought Argaty in 1916, unfortunately Thomas Henderson died only six months after taking over the estate. Mrs Henderson, or the Gray Lady as she was sometimes called, was left to run the estate and bring up her children. She did that successfully, and was also very active in the community; in 1924 she gave the Rural Hall to the SWRI, the Earl of Moray allowing his land to be used for the building.

In due course Mr D.C. Bowser and Mrs M. Bowser, Mrs Henderson's daughter and son-in-law, took over the estate. This photograph shows their permanent arrival at Argaty in 1929, with all the house staff waiting formally to greet their new laird. On the extreme right of the photograph is J.W. Barty who was the factor, Mrs Bowser is holding Hope and Nanny Campbell is heading the line up.

The scene at the House gates as Mr and Mrs D. Bowser arrived, estate workers and farm staff forming a welcoming parade. The car arrived and the engine was turned off and ceremoniously pulled by the workers to the front door by rope! Third from left is John Maitland; sixth from left, John Campbell; sixth from right, John McCabe; third from right, Dalgleish, head gardener; far right, John McClaws.

In 1947 Capt. D. Bowser took over running the estate until 1986. Since 1982 Argaty House and the estate have been owned separately and Mr Niall Bowser and his wife Lynn now run the estate from Lerrocks Farm.

*Above:* The days before the motor mower around the early 1920s. Here, behind Argaty House, John McAlpine is at the front end with Jack McAnish guiding the roller. This shows how grass cutting was done without getting horse hoof prints in the grass. Note the special leather 'over shoes' the horse is wearing.

*Right:* Walter Grant, with gun, and friends return from a days' shoot. The dress has not changed much over the years. The jodhpurs are a little tighter on the thighs these days but the plus-fours remain the same.

The Argaty Engineers at work in the 'Dene'. This is a little dell that was maintained as a semi-wild garden, with quaint bridges and winding paths through the woods. Left to right: Jimmy Drummond, John McLaws, -?-, J. McCabe, -?-, John Maitland.

This scene of 'washday' on the Argaty estate, at the Netherton farm, would not have been such an unusual sight in the 1930s. Kate Croy makes the job of tramping blankets look like quite an elegant activity and Grandpa Croy, with hand on hip, is supervising. Does that ring any bells with you ladies out there?! The three children from left to right are Netty, Ian and George Croy.

The Gray Lady, Mrs Thomas Henderson of Argaty. She is remembered fondly for her energy in turning some of the wilderness of Argaty into a gardener's wonderland. The Garth, the Dene and the walled garden were all a credit to her ideas and hard work. She planted in excess of 30,000 bulbs around the house and said she got some of her inspiration from the sky, no doubt from the shadows and clouds. It was said her love of Argaty and her gardens was only surpassed by her love of her children and grandchildren, and her garden diary records how she planned her work and projects meticulously with knowledge and inspiration. Her generosity to the community in the shape of the Rural Hall is a lasting tribute to her memory.

Argaty Mill was originally a corn mill and later a bobbin mill, possibly associated with the Deanston Mill. When it was eventually demolished, the present house was built around 1959, when Mr and Mrs D.C. Bowser moved out of Argaty and into the new house. There are numerous accounts during the seventeenth century of the miller not honouring his obligations in providing grain to the laird, and the tenants not providing their quotas of corn to the mill or assisting with maintenance to the mill and the lade, and the consequences thereof!

Mother Bell and twin foals, Darling and Jean, at Netherton Farm on the Argaty estate. It is very unusual for any mare to carry twins to full term and even more rare for both to survive at birth and grow normally. These two are the exception to the rule.

## Moray Estate

Doune Lodge was built c.1802 by Francis, Lord Doune and later the 10th Earl of Moray, on the site of Cambuswallace House, which had belonged to the Edmonstones of Duntreath. Legend has it that it may have links to William Wallace. It is the local seat of the Earl of Moray, who purchased the site from the Edmonstones.

Cambuswallace was bought for two reasons. The first, in order to consolidate the Moray Estate of Doune into one block of land. Prior to the purchase, the estate was intersected by the Edmondstone property into two quite separate blocks. The second reason was that it provided an excellent site for a new house, the castle having been uninhabitied for many years. The last time a family was able to live there was in the early 1700s. Part of the old house of Cambuswallace was incorporated into the new house. The architect may well have been William Stirling.

The house was harled in 1912 and painted white. During the period 1932 to 1952 the house was leased to tenants. Then the present Earl took up residence, much to the delight of local people. The park and its gardens extend to some sixty acres, and for some years were open to the public as a delightful haven at the foot of the 'Braes'. The Doune Hill Climb attracts some thousands of visitors a year. The Doune Motor Museum, which was located in the Carse of Cambus steadings, was open for some thirty years and became a national landmark with its unique vintage collection and associated vintage shows, attracting thousands of visitors a year. These buildings are presently used as the Scottish Antiques & Arts Centre.

High up on the Braes, behind the house, is Severie which is known for the 'Judge's Seat'. Situated on a knoll in front of the farmhouse it commands a formidable view. Tradition has it that the people were judged at this stone and then, if found guilty, hanged at Kilbryde. Some think that this gathering of stones is more like a chair and may well have been some sacrificial altar, not to be confused with the Judge's Cairn, which is some distance south-east of the farm.

This remarkable photograph marks the cutting of the first sod for the creation of a new water supply for Doune from the Annat Burn. Prior to this, water was piped from tanks fed by springs in the Currachmore to several pumps. There were nine of these pumps in the village: one at Myrtle Cottage, one at the foot of Hall Lane, one near the Moray Institute, one at the north side of the Cross, one in Main Street at the corner of Moray Street, one in Moray Street, one in Kings Street, one near the Balhaldie Inn and one near the old steps of Terrace Cottage. Other private pumps were installed. Before these pumps the villagers relied on wells and the water of the Dragen and Ardoch Burns. This photograph, taken on the side of the Annat Burn just south of Essmitchell Cottage on 20 July 1899, marks the beginning of an era bringing a valuable water resource that changed the quality of daily life in Doune.

From left to right: Mr Mclean, solicitor; Mr Cairns, bailie (Commissioner); Mr Frater (plumber from Stirling); Mr James Innes, stonemason/builder; Mr Forbes, bailie; Revd Huie Bridge of Teith Church; Rev Mackay, Provost Presiding; Revd Peat, the manse; Countess of Moray, Doune Lodge; Captain R.M. Christie, engineer; Count of Moray; Mr McLaughlin, factor; Mr Tinlin Snr, bailie; Dr Andrew; Hugh Campbell; Mr Graham (Commissioner); Mr McDonald, draper; Mr Johnny Main (Commisioner).

A rather larger gathering at the same event shows Lady Moray with a number of estate workers and their children and some Doune residents. Almost 200 people are in this scene, which is remarkable in itself. They are all in their Sunday best and the children are particularly well

turned out. Considering they were in the middle of a field it must have been a nightmare keeping them clean till the proceedings were completed!

The magnificent old stable block and coach house shown here complete with clock tower and its original and unique 'black face', was built about 1812. It is thought that the architect was probably William Stirling of Dunblane. In the early years of the twentieth century it housed the famous Doune herd of Shorthorn cattle, which was dispensed with in the early 1930s. During the Second World War, the stable block was occupied by troops and there were ammunition dumps in the park. At the end of the war, Polish troops were based here awaiting return to Poland. The building also marks the entrance to the Moray estate home farm, the Milton, Calziebohalzie, Severie and Waterside farms, the High Braes and the High Wood, which conceals the famous Camp Stone.

The Mill at Burn of Cambus showing the old bridge in use around 1900, the house still stands today but the mill is not remembered by anyone. The old stone mill wheels still stand at the road end as a memorial to what was once a busy mill and thriving community. Evidence of the buildings beside the Annat Burn are still clearly visible.

Mr William Boyd Johnston outside the Annat farmhouse, complete with mini corn stack and Sunday best. The farmhouse is now a ruin, but this family farmed here for many years in the early part of the twentieth century. The magnificent views from the house include the site of the ancient Annat Chapel, Castle (House of Annat) and possibly a Monastery and ancient burial grounds. The remains of these ancient buildings are no longer visible on the pretty knolls on the north side of the Annat Burn.

This interesting aerial photograph shows Burn of Cambus, which was demolished when the A84 was improved. This was the old smiddy up until the mid-1950s and the last blacksmith was Mr Kinloch. Jimmy Ure was the previous blacksmith. The actual smiddy was on the right-hand side of the building beside the road and was probably a smiddy in the days of the fairs, catching all the trade from the northern route. In this photograph you can see the proximity of the railway to the cottages and the Annat Burn immediately behind the buildings, hidden by trees.

This is a view from the front of the same building at Burn of Cambus with Janet McIntosh at the door, taken around 1930. Burn of Cambus was a considerable settlement at one time prior to 1750, with two mills, the Burn of Cambus and Candy Mill at Kilmadock, two monasteries, one at Kilmadock and one two miles up the Annat Burn, near the Annat Castle. Now only two or three houses comprise the community.

A similar view some forty years later and the cottage has enlarged windows. This is Eddie Ross on guitar in 1970 – Janet McIntosh's grandson, the third generation of the same family to live at Kilmadock and Burn of Cambus.

This is the community of Old Kilmadock taken around 1972 a few years before it was demolished. It shows the River Teith and the Deanston Mill Lade running across the middle of the picture. Five or six families lived here only a few yards away from the Old Kilmadock graveyard (just to the right of the photograph) and possibly the site of one of the earliest Christian sites in Scotland. The old manse is at the far side of the courtyard that was used in the filming of Monty Python. It was also the site of a candy mill which has long since disappeared together with its lade, but some local people still remember the lade down the Annat glen.

This lovely poem written by Daisy McIntosh depicts the way of life these families enjoyed in this idyllic place.

### Old Kilmadock– Down Memory Lane

Old Kilmadock was a wonderful place
A beauty to behold,
It stood alone on the lea of the hill,
Protected from the strong winds and cold.

Where the river Teith goes ambling by,
It was a beautiful sight to see,
On the riverside grew,
Bluebells in great hue, and the wee white daisies and primroses sweet
Were scattered in profusion around our feet.

The air was filled with perfume sublime,
Believe me folks, that was a magical time,
They were happy and kindly,
The folks that lived there,
Their pleasures were simple but fun,
When the sun was high in the blue, blue sky,
We would picnic at the side of the burn.

I can hear again my mother say,
In her kind and gentle way,
'Sarah and Rab you carry the picnic bag,
Barbara you carry the kettle for tea,
Daisy you take wee Jimmy by the hand,
And come and follow me'

The two cats followed a wee bit behind,
Then Flossie ran up a tree,
Tibby was running about with a hump on her back,
Then came scurrying over to me.

When I think of the times,
When the weather was fine,
And we all sat around the old apple tree,
The cattle were grazing high up on the hill
And the grasshoppers were louping free,
The skylark on high singing up in the sky,
It did seem heaven to me.

The old house has gone now,
And the old folks too,
The people who lived there,
Were special but few.
They brought to the valley,
Contentment and joy,
A wee bit of heaven,
For each girl and boy.
Entwined in the laughter and love,
There were a few tears,
Which have all blown away
On the wind through the years.

So if you should pass by there,
Stop – and linger a while,
In the quiet of the valley,
Where the soft winds blow.

You may hear again, the echo,
Of children at play,
Laughing and running,
Around in the hay.

## Lanrick

The site of Lanrick Castle dates back at least 700 years and probably is much older given its link to the Kilmadock Chapels. The site of the Lanrick Chapel lies west of the castle and near some ancient yew trees. The present building has now become a ruin but was always the home of an influential family. The Earls of Menteith were resident for many years, which only changed in 1460 when the Earl's daughter married Sir John Haldane of Gleneagles. The estate and castle remained the seat of the Haldanes until 1785, when the estate was confiscated during the Jacobite rebellion.

The Wordie family was in residence for some years before the Macgregors purchased the estate and called the main house Castle Gregor. The uniquely-shaped Macgregor Monument was erected by this important family. The Jardines were the next owners, taking over in 1840, when William Jardine rebuilt what was to be considered a splendid example of the Scottish Baronial style of house complete with turrets, which gave the impression of castle-like status. It was possible to build such a grand building at this time because of the success the Jardine's had with their dealings in the opium trade. It was Sir Robert Jardine and his brother, Andrew, who sold the castle to the most recent owners, the Stroyans, who purchased the property in 1905. John Stroyan was a well-regarded MP for many years and the estate and castle remain in the family till this day although the castle has recently been pulled down.

The Stroyan family around 1936, when the castle was very much a family home with all the splendid trappings of success. The ballroom was full of chandeliers and mirrors and there are people who still remember working in the 'Big Hoose' with affection. It is thought that now one of the largest chandeliers adorns the Green Room at the White House in America. Others remember it as a classic big house with cold draughty places, a nightmare to keep warm and maintain.

From left to right, back row: Silvia Hasell, Margaret Hasell, Maureen Durville, Evelyn Stroyan, John R.A. Stroyan, Naomi McCaw, Sir Frank Newnes, John Sinclair, Miss Emily Stroyan, Alan Stroyan, Major Hasell, Miss Broughton (governess). Front row: John Stroyan MP, Sheila Stroyan, Mrs Edith Stroyan, Mrs G. Hasell, Lady Newnes.

Mr James Ure and Miss Sheila Stroyan outside the front door of Lanrick in the 1930s. This splendid photograph shows life in a different era, when hunting, shooting and fishing were serious pastimes for any estate owners. James Ure worked on the estate for some forty years and latterly was head gamekeeper.

Years ago, jiggers and gaffs were used by fishermen but were considered a bit rough. Those keen to earn a quick buck often used the technique of blasting pools with explosives, an outlawed but nevertheless effective method. Girning – snaring trout in a horsehair noose at the end of a stick is a very old-fashioned method. Guddling or tickling trout is still a favourite with children. The Blair Drumond estate used salmon traps, or cruves, downstream below the castle.

The Macgregor Monument a massive 60ft-high structure, like a very large and unusual tree stump which has had its branches and upper portion severed. Built in the early nineteenth century, it may be that it is a statement about a very influential family whose name was proscribed but who in spite of all their misfortunes and difficulties never lost their status and power.

A very proud member of the Stroyan family shows off a Christmas present, taken c.1905.

## Gartincaber

This estate was very important for many years, being the home of the ancient family of Dog, which had long and powerful associations with this area. The name means grove on a hillside. The impressive avenue of lime trees was planted in 1747 and exists to this day.

The Gartincaber Tower is a very well-known landmark and anyone passing near it will always remark: What is that? What does it signify? They may well ask because it does have a tale to tell. It was built as a dovecot, a 'ducket' for the housekeeper of the house, but it is said to mark the centre of Scotland. This is much debated to this day and indeed, if you try various experiments, you may come near to this point. How do you find the centre of a country that has a very irregular coastline, with hundreds of islands and land masses that lie miles offshore? Does anyone know the answer or is it a matter of informed opinion?! It could be – but it is unlikely – that it is in the area that is the centre of Scotland. That is the only answer I can come up with; you will have your own opinion. There is no doubt that this is an impressive landmark and if it gets people talking about the issue then it has served a lasting purpose!

# Nine
# Around Doune Village

**Schools**

We know there was at least one school in Doune in 1653 and in the 1750s there were schools at Lanrick, Torrie and Colvoie on the Coillechat Burn. By 1831 there were eight schools in the Parish: one parish school in Doune and two private schools. There was a private school at Buchany with thirty-nine children, which seems remarkable and points to its having been quite a large community at that time. There were private schools at both Drumviach, which existed until 1943, and Bridge of Goody and two mill schools in Deanston. The total number of children in all those schools at that time was over 500 pupils, but we have to remember there were no secondary schools as such in those days.

The Doune Parish School in Moray Street was the first purpose-built school. It was erected in 1854 and was used initially just for the younger pupils. In 1898 the parish school was enlarged and improved.

The east Free Church school was erected in 1846 beside the Mains Farm, and was sold in 1894.

The present new school, built on the site of the Roman fort, cost £80,000 and was opened on 26 March 1969 by Major D.C. Bowser CBE of Argaty.

**Grossett Fair**

The gala day of today has its origins in the Grosset Fair which links back to the Gooseberry Fair which was held on 26 July and was, in the eighteenth century, mainly for the sale of cattle, general business and hirings. It was one of six extremely busy fairs throughout the year, at one time second only to Falkirk in size in the whole of Scotland.

For more information about the fairs, see Chapter Four.

*Opposite:* The entertainment at the Cross. Two keen performers doing a turn with a large gathering of onlookers. This stage was brought out every year together with the piano, bunting and lights. It may prove a little hazardous these days with the traffic that flows through Doune today.

Getting ready for the procession, Jimmy Croy at the helm around 1930. The gala day started in July 1937. It is now held in June each year. The war years were the only interlude. Since then it has been an annual event with the crowning of the Queen and a procession through the village of Doune. It used to be a week-long affair, but has dwindled in recent years to a one-day event. Proceeds still go towards giving the old folk a good time with visits and entertainment.

Crowning of the Gala Queen, Mona MacDonald, in 1954. From left to right, back row: May Bruce, Evelyn Millar, Thea Taylor, Barbara Fox, Margaret Baird, Peter Stirrit, Isobel Ferguson, Mrs J. Rintoul, Jane Grant, Lesley -?-, Effie Drummond, Wilma Dick, Chrissie Campbell. Front row: Billy Campbell, -?-, Elizabeth McLaws, -?- Brown/Morrison, Mary Samson, Billy Lothion, Queen Mona McDonald, Doreen Bruce, -?- Burnett, Margaret Morrison, Aileen Maclon, Margaret Drummond, William Dick/David Wilson.

This five-ton Bedford does the honours in carrying the Queen and her attendants, and no longer the horse and cart; showing the changing times. From left : Steve McAlpine, Olive Innes.

*Right:* Gala Queen Rosemary Ross, being crowned by Mrs Bain c.1951/1952. Ella Kirkwood is back left with Mr W. Muckersie, Headmaster of Doune Primary, in the background.

*Below:* A magnificent model of the *Queen Mary*, made by William Hunter of the Red Lion, with sailor boys Carl Hunter, left, and John Bain, right, in 1937; the whole of the inside of the boat lit up. This shows how much effort was put into making this a notable event.

This charming family photograph shows how much a family event the gala day was. Here the MacKenzie family shows off their fancy dress in the Moray Park. From left to right Jean, Ellen, Michael, Henry, Mary. In the background are some of the twenty-one lime trees planted around the park to commemorate the coming of age of Lord Doune in 1913.

This photograph was taken in the Moray Park, with Jane and Audrey Croy on the Jubilee seat and the school in the background. It is easy to see why the Croy family always did well in the Gala Day fancy dress events.

The first Provost of Doune was Robert Main in 1890, when Doune's status as Police Burgh was established. This status existed until 1975 when the village came under County Council control. The last provost was Ian Bain. During this time administration was carried out with the Provost, two Baillies, six Councillors, a Town Clerk, a Town Chamberlain, a Burgh Surveyor and a Registrar.

*Above:* Presentation on 25 May 1937 to Provost John MacFarlane of the Provost's chain of Office. From left to right:
Sir A.K. Muir, ex-Provost J. McAnish, J. Dykes, Senior Baillie Morrison, Lady Muir, Councillor Blacklock ex-Provost, Provost MacFarlane (veterinary surgeon, Doune), Revd D. Duncan, Sir W. McNair-Snadden.

*Right:* Willie Docherty wearing his chains of office as Provost in 1961/62 with his invitation to the Palace of Holyroodhouse. A keen footballer, like his father before him, his son Willie keeps up the family tradition.

This old sawmill was opposite Golden Acre, next to the Parton Muir, around 1930. This sawmill converted timber for use in coalmines. No evidence of its existence can be seen on the ground. The area is now part of the Wood of Doune and planted with trees.

The Brig O' Balkerach, as this fork in the road is known, about the time of the coming of age of Lord Doune, 1913. The cart belongs to Murray the coal merchant. The old station can be seen over the wall, along with the distinctive spire of the West Church.

*Opposite:* Aldo Togneri on his ice cream cart taken in front of the café in Balkerach Street. The area around the corner at the foot of Hall Lane was the first bit of pavement to be concreted over when the council agreed to take over maintenance. The old whin sets therefore soon vanished from both the Main Street and Balkerach Street.

This scene depicts an annual event, which unfortunately has ceased due to the traffic, no doubt. A very proud and brave mother swan leading her cygnets down Moray Street to the Ardoch and the Teith to begin their adult life after leaving the nursery of the ponds. Three-year-old Margaret Ann Taylor looks on in 1963 under the watchful eye of Douglas. Springbank's lorries are forced to take a slower pace than usual!

## David Calder & Sons in Business 1926-1985

David Calder opened the bakery in 1926 at 68 Main Street, which was the shop and the bake house. The elder son, Robert, became involved after serving his apprenticeship with Graham, the baker at the Cross (in the building now occupied by Clan Books) under the foreman George Martin, from Buchany. In those days an apprenticeship was seven years for a bread baker and five years for a pastry baker.

Over the years Allan and John became involved in their father's business. They are seen here on their father's cart outside 68 Main Street, with Mary pulling the cart and David at the helm. John tells the tale of cutting his driving teeth with a delivery of a wedding cake by jig to Thornhill. He was thirteen years old at the time and succeeded in making the delivery intact. His father then decided he had passed the test and allowed him to drive the van. This was called a nine-board van because it held nine boards of bread which each held eighteen dozen half loaves. It was not uncommon for local families to have four boards a week to slice – sliced bread did not come in till the 1930s. By 1939 the company was delivering to Deanston, Thornhill, Ruskie and part of Dunblane as well as covering the immediate area around Doune.

In 1940 Allan joined the Army, and in 1941 John followed. Bob who was at the time the only man in the area who could do Morse code, joined the Observer Corps. During the war the area was full of army personnel and, in a bid to help, Annie, David's wife, and sister Margaret opened a tearoom at 68 Main Street.

The nine-board van in Castlehill with David Calder at the helm. Also seen in the photograph are some of the Elder and Fyfe banana boxes outside Jock McTurk's house.

After the war the boys returned to the business. In 1946 Allan started the fruit business almost by accident, after John had saved an unmanageable horse, Donald, from the butcher for £25, seen in this photograph at the top of George Street. Then someone suggested the need for a fruit van, and after some expert management, the horse went on to pull the fruit cart successfully for many years. In 1953 the family acquired the shop at 13-17 Main Street, which John's devoted wife Isa ran for twenty-seven years. David had to retire from the bakery in the 1960s due to bad health. The business continued until 1985 when John Calder retired.

This fascinating photograph tells a unique story of how Doune's community, like others between Doune and Loch Lomond, did their bit to haul the SS *Sir Walter Scott* over the rugged terrain of Glen Arklet from Loch Lomond to Loch Katrine. The exact details are hard to establish but it seems to have been in the summer of 1899. Each community was given the opportunity to raise a team of horses for three weeks. No doubt they were paid accordingly. These horses pictured at the Bridge of Balkerach (the junction of the A84 with the A820) had returned from this feat and celebrated their return with this photograph. Only one person has been positively identified so far, John McIntosh (Jock the Laird), seventh from the left. It is his son, Jimmy

McIntosh, who verifies this piece of oral history. It may be that Murray the coalman's horses were used and he is in the group. Woodside Cottage can be seen on the far left of the photograph. There would have been no Muir Hall, and no Wood of Doune, but the Woodside, an established inn, was well frequented and would no doubt have been the next port of call!

In 1581 King James VI ordered that the Wood of Doune be surrounded by a dyke, the 'wod dyk', to protect his favourite hunting ground. The dyke was 9ft high, 15ft at the base and 2½ft wide at the top. The photograph shows a smaller dyke, but evidence of a high mound can still be seen in this picture. The wood was known as the Park of Doune in 1724.

*Opposite*: Balkerach Street Doune around 1905, looking north-west towards Callander. You can see the last thatched house in Doune on the left. Unfortunately the roof fell in during the 1930s when Mrs Bridget McLeod lived there. During the 1800s most of Doune was thatched, including most of Balkerach Street, the west side of Queen Street, the east end of Main Street and Moray Street. These houses were generally on one level. It is thought that the name Balkerach comes from hen and may be linked to a farm, which was around the present Woodside Cottage. It is also thought that it is the newer end of Olde Doune, which may well have been slightly separated from the Doune, that originated down at the Ardoch. On the right of this picture was a mark in the pavement that marked the site of the old well, it lies in front of the present day bus shelter. The plague hit Doune between 1640 and 1650 and it was thought this well was partly responsible! The door on the immediate right of the picture became the Italian Café, selling ice cream and chips.

Trossachs Pier and S.S. "Sir Walter Scott"

### The SS *Sir Walter Scott*'s relationship with Doune

What, you may say has the SS *Sir Walter Scott* got to do with Doune and Deanston? The previous picture tells the story. Kilmadock sent a team of horses to transport her in sections from Loch Lomond to Loch Katrine in the summer of 1899. The steam ship, built by William Denny & Brothers in Dumbarton, cost £4,250 to build and in fact over half her final cost, £2,228, went in transport costs. She was built in knock-down form so she could be transported by barge up Loch Lomond then by horse and cart over the hills to Loch Katrine, where she was finally assembled. She was a screw steamer and today she is still powered by the original triple expansion steam engine, built by Matthew Paul & Co., engineers from Dumbarton. In this respect she is unique, as most comparable steamers have been converted to oil fired propulsion. The reason for its retention is to minimise pollution on what is basically Glasgow's water supply. Up to 120 million gallons a day can be transported along the aqueducts from Stronachlachar. The picture above shows her in her original form without wheelhouse and before the round portholes were introduced. Seen behind the *Sir Walter Scott* is the paddle steamer, *Rob Roy II*, her predecessor that was launched in the mid-1850s.

Harry MacKenzie, or 'Harry the Barber', outside the barber shop which he took over in 1927/1928. His father, Karl Gebelmann, came to Doune in 1921, offering a full range of hairdressing services, including 'vibratory treatment, bobbing, shingling, singeing, pointing and marcel waving with guaranteed satisfaction'. The family of eight children, Henry, Bernard (who died before they moved to Doune), Grace, Harold, Doris, Martha, Freddy and Sandy followed a couple of years later, and lived in No.47, next door to the business.

The Hunter Family; George Walkinshaw Hunter, his wife Helen Christina, children Carl, Helen and William, outside the Red Lion Hotel in Balkerach Street about 1909. To the left of the picture the writing on the archway says, interestingly, 'Motoring – Stabling!' This is said to be the site of the first motor garage in Doune and had one of the first petrol pumps, a hand-cranked pump, which was situated under the archway on the wall of the Hotel. The fuel tank was underneath the room in the hotel known as the public hall! During the war, the army requisitioned the hall, and some forty soldiers were billeted there, and the garage became a dining hall. On one occasion a Bren Gun Carrier stopped, which caused quite an upheaval. Through all this the hotel enjoyed a brisk trade, beer came by motor lorry, but the spirits came via Midland Scottish Railway via the railway station and was brought by horse and cart to the hotel, custom-sealed in wooden boxes, which had to be returned. The Hunter family had the Red Lion for over 125 years, and saw the days of the coaches evolve through to the new age of the motor car. The coaching station was at the back and side of the hotel, and the first motorised post vans in the area were based there.

Robert Ainslie in the butchers yard at the Smiddy, Main Street, around 1933, Leo McLaughlin is leaning out of the window. Robert had a butcher's shop at the corner of Balkerach Street and the Cross, and also sold fruit and vegetables. Robert's father (also called Robert Ainslie) had the antique business at the old Smiddy for many years.

The Cross at the centre of Doune looking down towards the top of George Street, formerly known as Pudden Wynd, because of the number of butcher shops that sold black and white puddings. Later it was known as Chapel Street, because of the two churches. It was renamed George Street after the Revd George Mackay who built a block of houses at the top of the hill. The status bestowed on the village as a Burgh of Barony in 1611 gave the Earl of Moray the right to erect a cross. This was a point at which the formal business of the Burgh was conducted. It is a much debated point that the Cross may have stood in front of the first Kilmadock church which stood further back from the road than the present church seen below at the end of Main Street. That would have been nearer the centre of Olde Doune than the present location. It was probably a less grand affair, just a pillar set in a large stone.

It also seems that the Cross was built on the site of an old stable, and excavation around the base of the Cross, during the 1940s, revealed cobbles, straw, chaff and horse dung making this theory more likely. You can also see quite clearly in this photograph the old water pump, one of nine in and around Doune, and the weighbridge.

Looking down Main Street around 1900. The road surface is a dirt track although the pavement is made up with whin sets. Apart from the alterations to the Balhaldie and the road being tarred, the buildings are all very recognizable. The lane down the side of the Mile End was just wide enough for a small lorry and the Gardiners, who had the first lorry in the area, regularly took pigs to market. This became an event which the local lads loved as it often meant piglet chasing up the street when the odd 'escapee' had to be caught! John Blackwood remembers this amusing activity fondly.

A well-known local character, Dan Kennedy was best remembered as a poet, he indulged in both local themes and personal, topical oratories. One such poem was about Duncan Dow who stayed in the Keepers cottage at the Brig O 'Teith and terrorised the local lads and lassies. The hill down to the bridge is called Dan Doo's Brae after Duncan Dow. Dan Kennedy lived at Glengarry Cottage, 68 Main Street, and when he was not writing poems he was slating roofs. Doune seemed to be well-known for slaters for some unexplained reason.

An unusual view of Main Street and the Cross, from the Kilmadock Parish Church. In the mid-nineteenth century there were fourteen inns in the parish, eleven in Doune, one at Burn of Cambus, one at Drumvaich and one at Deanston. In Doune a number of houses were inns but were little more than rooms, which sold drink; no sleeping accommodation or food was available in the majority. The Rob Roy Inn was near the Star Inn (also once known as the Doune Castle Hotel and Head Inn, and situated where the Mile End is now), while the Black Bull was at the foot of George Street on the south side. Other inns included one between the Mile End and Castlehill Road, another which was McFarlane's house, the White House at No.32 Main Street, and one other which might have been near Caddell's pistol factory or behind the Balhaldie. The Woodside, the Red Lion and the Balhaldie survive to this day, the Highland Hotel being the most modern of all. At the end of the eighteenth century there could have been another seven inns. Certainly in 1822 Doune had thirteen watering holes.

One must always remember that, during the early nineteenth century there was a number of illicit stills in and around the district, especially on the 'Braes' where smuggling of the water of life was a way of life. The Doune fairs, the pistol business and the mill at Deanston all gave this part of the world a very busy ambiance.

The Woodside Hotel at the end of the nineteenth century. The green from which this photograph was taken was common ground and used as a drying or bleaching green, and ran right along the roadside towards the Dragen Burn.

This is an early picture of the Malt Barn, also known as Terrace Cottage. This shows the double steps on to the road, which are still intact. There was a fleshers yard at the back of this area and a cooper's business just a few hundred yards down on the right near the Bridge of Ardoch.

This view, from the other side of the Malt Barn, shows how the steps were double-sided, and how the building may well have extended along the built-up banking (see map on page 11). It is thought that there may have been a kiln in this area, which could have been linked to the making of glass balls for the sport of Glass Ball Shooting, the early sport of Clay Pigeon shooting. Doune has always been renowned for its fine quality sand, which is very pure and ideal for glass making.

Queen Street, formerly known as Kilerse, around 1920 before the council houses were built. It was renamed Queen Street after the McQueen family of Terrace Cottage. The name Kilerse has associations with a kiln, which local people believe was in the area, certainly the Malt Barn may have used one. The area was also referred to as Kilcarse and Kilarch. One quaint story is about a young girl who was embarrassed about the name Kilerse, and when asked by the local minister where she lived, said 'Kilmadoup', thinking it more refined.

The Muir Hall was completed in 1922 when it was also used as the Burgh Offices. The hall has been used by numerous groups, for countless festivities, over the years. Here a Christmas event is celebrated around 1961/62. This annual event was run by Sam Blackwood, of the Doune Football Club.

From left to right, front row: Mr Young, Mrs Young, D. Hooks, Mrs White, Mrs Prentice, Mrs Fox, Mrs Gillies, D. Martin, J. Bissett, Mrs Bissett, Mrs Sharp, Mrs Martin, K. McKenzie, -?-. Second row: Mrs Hill, Mrs Duncan, Mrs Connelly, Mrs Murray, -?-,Miss P. Connelly, Mrs Inglis, Miss Morris, Mrs McLaggan, Mrs McLeod, Mrs Donnelly, Mrs Duncan, Mrs Mitchell, Mrs Mallon, Mrs McDonald, A. Sinton, Miss Main, Mrs R. McKenzie, Mrs Marshall. Third row: Mrs Smith, Mrs Morrison, Mary Connelly, Mrs McAlpine, Mrs Campbell, Miss Bond, Mrs McTurk, D. Crombie, Mrs Docherty, -?-, J. Mitchell, Mr Masterton, A. Duncan, E. Fox. Forth row: -?-, D. McTurk, Revd R. Watt, W. Docherty, Fr Purceli, Revd Hutchison, Mr McKenzie, Jimmuck Ferguson. Back row: J. Duncan, W. Murray, -?-, W. McLeod, Agnes Kelly, Peter Kelly, S. McIntosh, J. Potts, W. Watson.

The Bridge O'Teith has a very interesting story attached to it and there has even a play written around the story. Before 1535 there was no bridge, just a ford and a ferry, and when Robert Spittal, who was an accomplished tailor to royalty, found himself at the ferry without any money having mislaid his purse, he was refused passage. For whatever reason, as a result he decided to fund the building of the present bridge just as he built other bridges and provided Stirling with a hospital. There is no doubt he was a very public spirited individual. Sometimes it is called the Scissors Bridge, and there is a shield on the parapet of the bridge with an inscription to the tailor together with engraved scissors. A fine bridge to start off with, it was widened and repaired in 1866 and more recently it has been improved, resulting in the level of the road being raised, partly obscuring the inscription.

A gypsy camp-out beside the River Teith in 1861. It looks a very orderly site and has an air of enchantment about it.

# Ten
# Scenes around Deanston

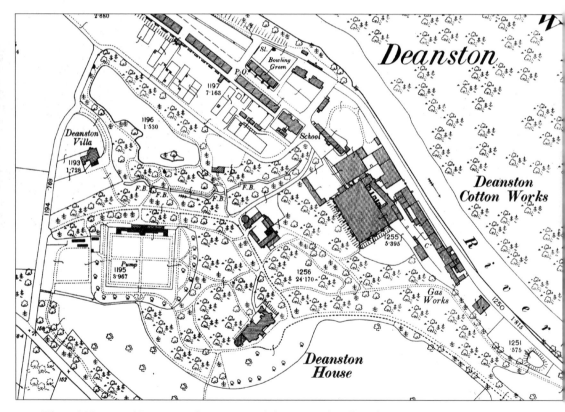

This 1900 map of Deanston shows most of the original mill and associated buildings. You can see the man-made lake beside Deanston Villa, as well as the Divisions and the bowling green beside the first Division. It shows the new school and the old school in the mill grounds, together with the hall and library. Tullochan Knowe, the area used for the first recorded football matches, can be seen at the bottom right-hand corner.

## DEANSTON

The name Deanston comes from Walter Drummond who was Dean of Dunblane and took over the feu of the land from the Haldanes of Lanrick some time in 1500. Stobie's map of 1783 shows the village called Deans Town. Running along and past the present Chain Lodge on the south side of the Stirling road, lies the origins of Deanston. A row of cottages built around 1790 by William Murdoch of Gartincaber, originally called Murdochstown after the builder, housed around 250 mill workers. Eventually, for obvious reasons the nickname 'Cotton Row' became the popular name. These cottages were all pulled down around 1830, some twelve years after the Deanston Company bought most of Deanston, and the population of the village had risen to over 500. Deanston was born.

Murdochstown (on the extreme left), showing its position in relation to the bridge and the castle. In 1818 the whole of this area was sold to the Deanston Company. Deanston village grew up and around the mill, which was erected in 1785 by the Buchanan Brothers of Carston. Prior to that, there was probably only a scattering of dwellings and a flax mill in this area.

Archibald Buchanan was only sixteen when he became manager, but the family had links with the Manchester cotton industry and had been linen yarn merchants. Benjamin Flounders, a Yorkshire Quaker, bought the mill in 1793 and owned it until around 1807. The mill survived a fire in 1799, but around twenty families left the area as a result. After a turbulent period, the mill closed for a few years in the early nineteenth century. However, rescue was soon to come around 1808 when James Finlay & Co. took over and developed something of an icon of its day; an orderly, prosperous village with a population cared for by its employers. James Finlay would not allow a public house in the village. The mill was known as the Adelphi Mill in the early days and inevitably the name stuck. Not unlike New Lanark in many ways, the forward thinking new way of treating the workforce resulted in an establishment that lasted over 180 years, through the industrial revolution and into the new age of steam, railways, gas, cars, electricity, television, airplanes and men landing on the moon!

# James Smith

The business of the mill had to move with the times to survive, but not only did it do that, it kept ahead of the game. In 1807 James Smith, who was related to the Buchanans, had just what it took to become the first mill manager at the age of only seventeen. He grew with the business and created a model of efficiency, continually improving production processes. By 1840 Smith had increased the output of the mill to a level that required over 1,000 workers, who were drawn not just from Doune and Deanston but also from Thornhill, Callander and the Stirling area. The formidable mill lade, 1,608 yards in length, and the embankment wall had been built, as had the Lanrick dam that fed the lade. A unique weaving shed was also built, which had a cast iron 'Cupola' roof covered with earth for insulation, which proved very effective and efficient. This large complex of buildings had various underground passageways to ease the industrial processes and maintenance of the site. Everything was done to make the mill more efficient and therefore more viable.

Over its history Deanston has made many different types of cotton goods including curtain lace, cotton stylised sheets and towelling for many great institutions, using complicated jacquard looms. By the end of each day cotton cloth was sent to Catrine, the sister mill, for finishing.

One of the by-products of the mills was that Deanston enjoyed the benefits of gas before any other village in Scotland and ahead of all the major cities. It is said that Westminster Bridge was lit in 1913, the same year that Deanston enjoyed gas; it was some forty-five years later that Doune got gas!

James Smith has gone down in history, not only for his weaving mechanisations, but his other successful ventures, including bridge design. He not only designed the Lanrick Bridge, but invented a deep soil drainage system named 'Deanstonisation' and was an advocate of deep ploughing, which revolutionised the reclaiming of bog and marsh areas. In conjunction with this he also invented a reaping machine and a salmon ladder. He built what was known as a model farm to demonstrate these various inventions behind the mill and people still remember the model hut up behind the Divisions, as shown on the map on page 112. In fact, when Mr Smith retired from the mill in 1841 it was to concentrate on his agricultural ventures. He died nine years later, a credit to his profession. He is buried in the old Kilmadock Churchyard on the banks of the Teith within sight of the old mill and lade.

In 1831 Deanston had three grocers shops, one haberdashery and there were another two grocers at Bridge of Teith. Schooling by a shift system run by the James Finlay Co. allowed 140 pupils to be taught in the village at this time.

In 1862 the mill hit on hard times, partly due to the American situation when there was no raw cotton available, but it is commendable that the owners continued to pay the workforce half-pay and utilised the down time to increase the education available. The whole of the wage bill at that time was £13,000, showing a remarkable social responsibility.

It was also at this time that Sir John Muir became a partner; he was already an entrepreneur in tea and cotton. He opened the Deanston Hall to the public in 1891. Six years later, in 1897, the old part of the present school was built and the Old Mill School was converted into a reading and recreation room. Sadly, the Deanston Hall closed in 1934.

Above are two of the four famous waterwheels that had been designed by James Smith. The first were installed and inaugurated in 1830. *Hercules*, the last wheel, was installed in 1833. All wheels were made at the mill foundry, and the oldest turned for 120 years, seen here with the vast water pipes that carried the lade water up to overshoot the wheels to give the maximum thrust and power. Water can be seen cascading down the wheels on the left of the picture. In 1945 the more efficient turbines replaced the massive wheels, which were some 36ft in diameter and 11ft or so wide, it was a sad but inevitable step forward. *Hercules* was said at the time to be the largest waterwheel in Europe, and the second largest in the world.

Aerial view of Deanston Mills before reconstruction showing Deanston House in the background on the left; the first of the council houses can be seen in the right-hand corner of the picture. Further cottages and semi-detached houses were built and, eventually in 1950, the County Council built a housing scheme of seventy houses. It was about this time that a new weaving shed was built. It was a sad day indeed, when, in January 1965, the workers were told that the mill would close on 2 April 1965. It was in that same year that some scenes of Dr Finlay's casebook were filmed in Deanston.

The Deanston distillery opened in 1966, when the Mill closed, after extensive internal refurbishment to accommodate the new industrial processes. One of the great strengths of Deanston, apart from the scenery, is the fact that an abundance of water means that it is one of the few distilleries that is completely self-sufficient in power, thanks to the Teith and the lade. Today there are four pot stills capable of distilling three million litres of alcohol a year! Burn Stewart purchased the property in 1990 and have developed rapidly since then, opening its second malt whisky distillery in Tobermory.

Deanston Mill taken around 1900 shows the old part of the buildings from the back. The six-storey red sandstone building, on the left of the photograph, was latterly known as the 'flats'. Raw cotton entered on the ground floor and by the time it left the top floor it had been made into thread. Each storey had nine windows, and in 1847 it is noted that 300 looms were in one apartment called the 'Arches' all run by waterpower. The bell tower sounded the beginning and ends of the shifts. The 'ware' area is seen in the middle of the picture between the bell tower building and the sandstone building.

The main mill buildings, as they looked around 1900. The picture gives a good impression of this large and solid, mainly sandstone, structure, and how it could easily accommodate over 1,000 workers. The buildings nearest the camera are demolished now. The main workers' entrance can just be made out between the tall sandstone building and the four-storey building

This view of Deanston is taken from the mill buildings around 1930. The car was not so popular then and the new school was about thirty-three years old. You can see the bowling green beside the lade, with the bowling hut behind the trees. The lade runs under the bowling green, under the old hall and schoolhouse. With a discerning eye and a magnifier you can see Old Kilmadock across the river centre-right between the trees. The line of mill houses at the centre-bottom has been demolished. In that line of houses going up from the centre of the picture are the old school house, the library and hall. The hall was opened by Sir John Muir in 1891 and closed in 1934. The house with the greenhouse-type roof, in the bottom left-hand corner, is the wheelhouse, and still exists today. Behind the Second Division you can see the washhouses, and at the end of that Division is the larger washhouse for the other Divisions. The first two Divisions were the first to be built, around 1811, followed by the final three around 1820.

John Grierson, who pioneered the documentary genre, was born in the mill schoolhouse on 26 April 1898; his father was the headmaster at the time.

Deanston, with this workforce, was able to put on a formidable display of loyalty to the crown when Queen Victoria toured the area in 1842. This was described as:

*A very interesting spectacle of the whole of the people and children employed by the great Deanston Cotton works, to the number 1,500, most of them with flags and pennons in their hands, who had been marched hither and drawn up in the field on the left of the road, the men on one flank and the women on the other, with the word 'industry' on their banners and their ban of music in the centre.*

It seems they were standing on a piece of elevated ground just south of Dunblane near to where Mr Stirling of Keir was ready to greet Her Majesty at the grand entrance to his estate, with the motto on a banner 'Farewell to Perthshire, Scotland's Queen'. Mr Smith of Deanston was part of the organizing party. It must have been quite a feat to organise a well turned out group of 1,500, some four or five miles from their homes!

This dam was locally known as the 'strip' and ran at a forty-five degree angle across the Teith towards Kilmadock. It was this dam that was used to store the volume of water for the massive waterwheel which sat at the end of the dam below the lade at river level. The original dam probably pre-dates the Buchanan buildings as there was an old flax mill on this site and the dam may well have been in use then. The children used to run back and forward on the 'strip', and it was always a bit of a hazard, especially when the river was running high. It was recently almost completely demolished and only a small bit of the east side remains. Now that the water is not held back unnaturally, the level of the Teith is now lower, showing how this would have been a favoured crossing. It is recorded as having been a ford before the mill lade was built when the embankment would have been a barrier to any access from the west side.

These two little girls are admiring the salmon ladder at the Lade dam, or Lanrick dam as it was known, which was built during 1825/1826 on the Teith. It is often called the Lanrick dam because of its proximity to the estate and castle.

The Divisions that housed many of the mill workers was, in its heyday, a fine example of good employment relations.In the early years, the Divisions had four levels of acccommodation, including a basement and an attic. The drying greens are well used and in the distance you can see the little bridge across the lade on to the path that the walker can take down to the dam.

*Opposite:* The walk up the side of the lade towards the lade mouth and Lanrick dam. A favourite walk for locals, it is some 25ft above the Teith in places and was a considerable feat to construct in its day. You can see the white house on the left, which is now demolished.

The school was built in 1897. In 1831 there were 140 pupils in Deanston between the evening and the day school. That was out of a population of 500. In 1915 there were only 103 children under Headmaster Keith Murray. The school was extended in 1926 to include cookery and woodwork rooms and by 1939 the roll had fallen to sixty-six. By 1948 the roll had fallen still further to thirty-four but in 1954 a school library opened and by the time the mill closed the school had fifty-three pupils on the roll under James Bain, Headmaster. These figures reflect the diminishing mill workers' population within the village.

A view from the other end of the cottages, or first Division as it was known, shows their unusual design, with the large mill buildings in the background. The clock tower was erected in memory of Lady Muir of Deanston. She always showed an interest in the well-being of Deanston people, right up until she died in 1929, and was always very generous in matters relating to the village. Allan Calder's vegetable cart can be seen on the left side of the picture.

Deanston was always very proud of its bowling green and the old Bowling Hut still stands, but the area is now generally used for allotments. The area was known as Lea Green and what was the first bowling pavilion was in fact used by the mill as a reading room and was used by the bowlers in the summer. The club was founded in 1880 and its emblem was a beehive, 'the hive of industry', the annual subscription was 4 shillings. The Ashworth Memorial Cup was donated by one of the mill managers and latterly was won for four consecutive years by Jim 'Tiger' Shaw. Mrs Blackwood can recall how her mother dispensed bowling scones from her back window beside the green. Not only did the mill care for the workers it looked after the bowling green and, within a year of the mill closing, the bowling club folded around 1966. The Lea Green houses were the homes reserved for the management team including the under manager, the works foreman and the head cashier. The manager usually lived in Deanston villa. Mr Cree was manager for thirty-six years followed by Mr Ashworth for twenty years and Mr Dearn from 1933.

One of the great bonuses of the mill was the way the workforce bonded and socialised together. For a great many years the two main shifts formed two distinct groups who had their own events and competed against each other in a very healthy way. This picture shows some of the good-looking lasses as the Tiller girls. From left to right: Anna Duncan, Agnes Kelly, Sadie Lauder, Betty Baird, Jean Marr, Nancy Reid, Ethel McLean.

A posh affair at the Mill – Concert. From left to right, back row: Agnes Morrison (Kelly), Hugh McLean, Betty Baird, Davey Lauder, Nancy Muir, Jim Marr, Billy Dunn, Jimuck, Hugh Muir, Jimmy Kelly, Jim 'Tiger' Shaw, Willie Cuthbert, Jean Marr, Sadie Lauder (Tough), Anna Cuthbert, George Scott, Florence McLean Jnr. Front row: Cathy Lauder (Tough), Elsie Matheson, Florence McLean Snr, Jessie Henderson, Betty Tough, Johnny Bowman.

Deanston House has an interesting history, seen here as it was in the early years of the nineteenth century. The Old House was the family seat of the Drummond's. It is thought that the original house was built around 1510 near the present house. It is from the Drummonds that Deanston got its name, as Walter Drummond was Dean of Dunblane – Dean's Town. The present building has had many uses, being first the home of James Smith, the Mill's first manager. Sir John and Lady Muir occupied the house but when Lady Muir died in 1929 it became a private school. Then, during the war, it was taken over by the Army. After the war it was taken over and restored and run for many years as a hotel. It is now a nursing home. When the hotel was opened it boasted a fine conservatory, which still exists today and can be seen on the far left of the picture.

This fine aerial view shows the splendid location that the house enjoyed through its history, with the River Teith and the Teith Bridge in the foreground. The old Teith Bridge manse and church are slightly obscured by the trees in the bottom left of the picture.

Deanston House staff on a night out in the hotel ballroom in the mid-1960s. From left to right, back row: Malcolm McLean Snr, -?-, Sadie Lauder, Mrs Anderson, Nelly Adams, Jimmy Duncan, Dot Adams, David Lidgate, Malcolm McLean Jnr, Danny Ludgate, Rita McLeod, Jimmy Anderson. Middle row: Ina Graham, -?-, Adam Lumsden, Mrs Lumsden, Denzel Crawford, Mrs Lidgate. Front row: Nancy McAlpine, Peggy McMaster, -?-, -?-, -?-, -?-.

This aerial photograph of the distillery shows a range of buildings that were almost all used by the mill. The old school can be seen top centre with the Deanston House grounds on the left. This was the mill in its last days after modernisation in the 1950s. The new buildings are those in the bottom half of the photograph. The buildings with greenhouse-type roofs are the old wheel houses. The building with the roof with the cupula windows is the weaving shed; its cast iron roof was once covered in earth for insulation.

Deanston looking towards the massive mill buildings along the first Division to the left and the second Division to the right.

'A Winter Walk' by Sandy Dickson at Croftinloan School, Form V, 1998 – Age twelve years.

I have brought this book to a close with what I feel is a most poignant painting that was done by twelve-year-old, Sandy Dickson of Lanrick. Sandy died in a tragic accident in a far-off land in the summer of 2000, while I was compiling this book. For the viewer this painting may mean different things, but to me it is like the journey through life, along a winter's path, which wynds through the unknown and unexpected, beautiful at times, cold at others. On a positive note, Sandy's death has led to the formation of the Sandpiper Trust. The Trust aims to raise money to go towards medical equipment for use in rural locations where it will provide much needed specialist medical assistance in the 'Golden Hour' that all-important time immediately after an accident. Sandy, his young life taken away cruelly too soon at fourteen, like young Johnny Ross who drowned at Kilmadock aged twenty-two months in 1949. They, like many others in our community over the years, are not forgotten and, like the past captured in old photographs, to be treasured forever.

# Bibliography

Barty A.B., *The History of Dunblane*
Baxter, Peter, *Football in Perthshire*
Black, *Picturesque Tourist of Scotland*
Fyfe, Alistair, *Scottish Inventors*
Kelvin, Martin, *The Scottish Pistol*
Mackay, Moray S., *Doune – Historical Notes*
Main, Lorna, *First Generations*
Maxwell, Gordon, *A Gathering of Eagles*
McCulloch, Stuart J., *Thornhill and its Environs – A Social History*
McKerracher, Archie, *The Street and Place Names of Dunblane & District*
McKerracher, Archie, *Perthshire in History & Legend*
Salter, Mike, *The Castles of the Heartland of Scotland*
Stewart, James, *The Settlements of Western Perthshire*
The first Statistical Account, 1799
The new Statistical Account, 1844